At His Appointed Time

At His Appointed Time

When God's Promises Are Suddenly Fulfilled

Pat Reynolds

Community Services Press
Washington, DC

Community Services Press
2101 N St., NW, Suite T-1
Washington, DC 20037

310-406-8300
www.communityservicespress.com

Copyright © 2014 Pat Reynolds

All rights reserved. No part of this publication may be reproduced or transmitted in any form or by any means, electronic or mechanical, including photocopying, recording, or by any information storage or retrieval system, without permission in writing from the publisher.

Printed in the United States of America
18 17 16 15 14   1 2 3 4 5

ISBN 13: 978-0-9841286-8-6

Editing by J. McCrary, CSP Editorial Services
Cover design by Nathelie Kelley
Interior layout by Westcom Associates

About the Cover Artwork:
There are five pickets in the open gate, the number of grace.
There are seven pickets in the fence, the number of completion.
The three steps represent Father, Son, and Holy Spirit.
The tree represents strength, shelter, and protection.

To my grandchildren

Kylan Chase Reynolds
Addie Elisabeth Reynolds
Harrison Boone Reynolds
Brenna Evin Reynolds
Hannah Grace Reynolds

More than anything, I want you, my grandchildren, to seek first the Kingdom of God and follow in His ways. I want your lives to reflect the life of Christ. I want you to know the joy of hearing God's voice and see Him do the impossible in your lives. I want God to be able to capture your hearts.

Since you were born, I have prayed hard for those things. It is to your honor that I dedicate this book. May you, too, know His Appointed Times!

Acknowledgments

To simply say thank you seems so insufficient, yet I offer my deepest gratitude to:

My husband, Charlie. Thank you for loving me, choosing me and believing in me. Without you, there would be no story! God knew you were my perfect helpmate and allowed us to walk this journey together.

Our children, Daman and Karri Anne, Tommy and Holly, for believing in us, even when we had no concrete reasons to give you for our leaving. You and your children have sacrificed along with us. Our journey is as much yours as it is ours.

Our Pastor, Tony Wofford, and our church family, Word Is Life of Snyder, Texas, for making sure, before we left for Guatemala, that we understood deep in our hearts that God had already provided all that we would ever need. God always provides, but He works through people to do it. We thank God that He has used the Word of Life Church as a vehicle for faithfully helping us to meet a mountain of needs throughout these years.

Pearlene Nolan, His Joy Ministries, for the thousand and one things you did in the early days, and continue to do, to help us keep His Appointed Time ministry operating. I can't recall one time when you said, "No, Pat, I can't do that." Your willingness to help has taken a huge load off our shoulders. God certainly knew whom to call.

Randy and Shauna Levens, our very first visitors in Guatemala. Everywhere I look in this ministry, I see your fingerprints and footprints. You have contributed to every aspect of the ministry. Thank you for being a part of God's vision for His Appointed Time Ministries and sharing what God has spoken to you.

Doug and Sherry Ryan. Charlie and I bless the day that we received a phone call from another missionary asking us to pick you up from the airport and let you spend the night at our house in Guatemala. From that day, we have been friends and partners in many areas of the ministry. You are constantly thinking of ways in which you can help. When I look at our vast view from the top of the mountain where Restoration Ministry sits today, I am overwhelmed at all that you have done to provide.

Gateway Church of Southlake, Texas. The first people to represent you to us were Doug Ryan and his daughter,

Katie, but they were not the last. Next came Juan and Anita Constantino and from there a host of Gateway team members. For most of our years in Guatemala, you have stood with us from the ministry to the police, the sponsorship of the children in Gerizim School, Freedom Ministry coming to minister to the missionary community at Restoration, to your recent donation that allows us to build a gymnasium for Gerizim Christian School, and install water filters and stoves in village houses. Thank you for allowing God to use you to help us minister in this great nation of Guatemala.

My aunt, Audine Bosher. As a young adult, I watched your love for the Lord and heard your stories of God's faithfulness; they gave me the desire to love and serve him with my whole heart. Rest assured, you taught me well!

There is not enough space to name all the individuals and churches that God has strategically placed on our journey. You have paid the bills, prayed for us, encouraged us to go on and given us hope and vision. Without you, His Appointed Time ministry would not exist. Even though your name is not in print, you know who you are. Even better, God knows who you are. Many of you have stood with us from day one. You have been the best mission board any two missionaries could hope for.

My Father God, the One who holds the keys to it all. To the One who saw me while I was being formed in my mother's womb. To the One who will receive me at the end of my journey. To the One who called me and gave me the strength to answer, "Yes, Lord, here am I, send me!"

Contents

Chapter One

Suddenly

For the vision is yet for an appointed time and it hastens to the end [fulfillment]; it will not deceive or disappoint. Though it tarry, wait [earnestly] for it, because it will surely come; it will not be behindhand on its appointed day.

Habakkuk 2:3 (Amplified Bible)

It was a hot morning in August, 1978, just another ordinary day in the Reynolds' household in Deming, New Mexico. Charlie left for his office at the First Baptist Church, where he was pastor. Our two boys, Daman and Tommy, walked across the street to school. I started my usual chores. As I sat on the floor in front of a pile of dirty laundry, sorting it into piles of whites, darks, towels, sheets and jeans, God thought it would be a perfect opportunity to surprise me with a word. At that point in my life, I wasn't accustomed to getting words from the Lord. God decided this needed to change, and this was the day that He chose.

As I sat among all those dirty socks, just an ordinary Baptist preacher's wife on an ordinary August day, God spoke a word that forever changed my life and the way that I would trust Him.

"Suddenly."

There were no audible voices and no bolts of lightning. There was no need. God can make Himself known in the most unusual places and He can speak as quietly as a church mouse. He certainly caught me off guard. My heart almost stopped. I knew that the God of the universe had stepped into my little space in order to share something of real importance with me.

It has been more than thirty-five years since God dropped *suddenly* into my spirit. I am sure He has spoken to many others, but I don't know if anyone has taken Him any more seriously than I did on that long-ago laundry day. I knew that I heard more than just a word; I knew that I received a promise from God. I didn't understand fully what *suddenly* was about, but I knew enough to believe God had something up His sleeve, and He had just shared a portion of it with me. What I didn't know was the strange turn of events that Charlie and I would walk down as we learned to live in the *suddenlies.*

When God first spoke *suddenly* to me, I made the normal human mistake that most of us make. *Suddenly* sounds like "*right now*!" I would learn in the following days, weeks and years that God's suddenlies and my suddenlies were quite different. A West Texas friend recently told me that her daughter was fixin' to have a baby. She stopped and corrected herself, "Well, I shouldn't say fixin', because it's still six months off." God can take years with *His* suddenlies.

God began a work in me that day, a work that has taught me to *wait* in Him. *Wait* and *suddenly* don't seem very compatible, but in God, I have learned, they are interchangeable. God's *suddenly* doesn't mean that it will happen immediately, but rather at His *appointed time.* You might have to wait months or years to get to the appointed time. Once His appointed time arrives though, it will happen quickly. He has taught me to hold on to His promises and believe His word no matter how long it takes, and He has chosen to use the suddenlies in my life to teach me.

I don't care much for waiting. I like the right here and now, and the sooner the better. God is not moved by that. He is not in a hurry. He is not on a time schedule like I am. I only have a few good years here on earth to do everything that needs to be done. You would think that

God would understand that and work with me. But here is the deal: He is after one thing in my life—just faith. *Faith in Him.* He wants me to walk in a faith that will believe Him over whatever I see or feel. Without that kind of faith, no matter what I do, I can't please Him, so says Hebrews 11:6.

In the following chapters, you will read about some of the suddenlies that have already taken place in my life, and you will read about the suddenly I am still awaiting. I pray that you will come to understand that God has some suddenlies for you too. Yours might come more quickly than mine; most likely, though, they will take time. Time is not the issue, not with God. He has all the time in the world. We are the only ones in a hurry. The issue is our faith in His word and His personal promises to us.

God wants us to learn to hold on to His promises so we can walk in the destiny that He has mapped out for our lives. In God's vocabulary, *suddenly* means *His appointed time.*

Chapter Two

Adversity

For our light and momentary troubles are achieving for us an eternal glory that far outweighs them all. So we fix our eyes not on what is seen, but on what is unseen, since what is seen is temporary, but what is unseen is eternal.

2 Corinthians 4: 17, 18 (New International Version)

In October, 1949, I had just turned three years old. I was like every other toddler, into everything and asking one question after another. Little did anybody know that my life was about to take a different turn.

My Aunt Ruth and I took the bus to Ft. Worth to have my picture taken. It was a long day of walking, so when I complained that my legs hurt, my aunt just picked me up and carried me without thinking much about it. By the time we got home, I was running a fever. My parents called the doctor, and he said to bring me in for a checkup.

The doctor examined me, said I just had a cold, and he prescribed baby aspirin and bed rest.

This portrait was taken the day I came down with polio--the last day I walked without braces and crutches.

At home, I took my baby aspirin as the doctor prescribed and climbed into bed. When I tried to get out of the bed the next morning, my body did not move. My parents rushed me to the hospital, where I was diagnosed with all three types of polio including Bulbar, which affects the lungs and is most often fatal. Polio affected every muscle in my body, and for the first few weeks, the only movements I could make were to open and close my eyes. The doctors told my family that there was no way that I could live. I shocked everyone when I didn't die, everyone but those who prayed and believed God could save my life.

I was in the hospital for four months, part of that time in an iron lung because I was unable to breathe on my own. The iron lung was used in pre-ventilator days to provide artificial respiration by expanding and contracting the ribcage.

When I finally breathed well enough on my own to go home, my parents gathered me up and we said our good-byes. My doctor had final words for my mother and daddy: *"You can either make an invalid out of her, or you can help her reach her potential. It is up to you!"* With those words ringing in my parents' ears, we headed home.

I was three and a half years old, and my little world was turned upside down. I began a lifetime being unable to walk without crutches. I returned home with braces from my neck down, on both legs, and little wooden crutches. Though I had undergone a great deal of change while I was in the hospital, one thing about me had not changed: I was the same determined, headstrong little girl I had always been! Polio may have robbed me of my ability to walk unaided, but praise God it did not steal my determination. God was going to take that part of my character and use it to help mold my life.

My determination showed up pretty quickly those first days back home. One day I decided that I wanted to go outside and I didn't want anybody to help me, either! I wanted to do it by myself. I needed to navigate two small steps once I opened the back door. I assessed the situation

Taken a couple of months before I was struck with polio, this snapshot shows the steps that I fell down and kept climbing back up. You can also see the gate my daddy stood behind as he watched me struggle with my crutches. That struggle was the catalyst for the way I'd handle many of the other battles in my life.

and knew that I could handle them. I started down the steps on my crutches, but before I knew it, I fell to the bottom. About that time, my daddy rounded the corner near the gate and saw me fall. His immediate reaction, as any parent's would be, was to run and pick me up. Then he remembered the doctor's words, *"Mr. Free, you can either help make an invalid out of your daughter or you can help her reach her potential."* With those words still ringing in his ears, Daddy stood really still, just behind the gate.

I wasn't hurt badly and was more scared than anything.

I am sure Daddy thought that would be the end of that, and he wouldn't have to give it another worry. But that was not how it was going to be; I was not going to give up that easily! I used my little wooden crutches to crawl and push myself up those stairs. By then the tears were rolling down Daddy's face. I didn't know it because he remained hidden from my view.

Again I positioned myself at the top of the steps—and again I fell, landing in the same position, flat on my face. My daddy didn't budge, but by now he was sobbing. This may sound hardhearted, but that wasn't the case at all. He was one of the most tenderhearted men I have ever known. That made his stillness even harder for him. Can you imagine how difficult it was for him to not run and pick me up?

For the second time, I pushed my crutches up and crawled back up the stairs myself. With all of the determination that a three-and-a-half year-old can muster, I started down those steps for the third time. I was not going to quit no matter how long it took. Those steps were not going to get the best of me. I was determined to be the winner! To my Father's delight (heavenly and earthly) I made it to the bottom without falling.
Daddy bounded through the gate with tears streaming down his face, and grabbed me, kissing and hugging me.

I told him all about what had just happened. I didn't have a clue that he had watched the whole thing. He was proud of me, not so much that I walked down two steps, but that I did not give up until I finished what I had set out to do.

I have come to realize that my daddy acted a lot like God that day. Those two steps would not be the end of my difficult situations. I have faced plenty since that day, and just like my daddy, my heavenly Father has been right there through them all. I have not always seen Him or felt Him, but He was there! He hasn't always run to pick me up either. It would not have been the best thing for me. There is far more at stake in my life than just saving me from pain and difficulty.

God doesn't want me, as His daughter, to be a spiritual invalid. He wants me to reach my potential in Him, so that together we can climb all of the steps we need to without falling or stumbling at every difficult turn in the road. In order to do that, there will be times that He has to remain very still and quiet, but close. God is wise enough to wait, and so was my dad.

Chapter Three

Hearing the Call

I pray that out of his glorious riches he may strengthen you with power through his Spirit in your inner being, so that Christ may dwell in your hearts through faith. And I pray that you, being rooted and established in love, may have power, together with all of the Lord's holy people, to grasp how wide and long and high and deep is the love of Christ.

Ephesians 3:16-18 (New International Version)

When I was about thirteen years old, I began to know in my spirit that God was placing a call on my life. The word "missionary" came through loud and clear. I don't recall any one thing that sparked it. I just started sensing the word "missionary" in my spirit. I wonder if sometime long ago there was a missionary in my family line who prayed for someone in our family to hear the call for missions. I don't know about the missionary, but I do know several members of my family have prayed for me throughout my life that God's sovereign hand would be over me and that my life would be spent in service to Him.

As I sensed God's call to missions, I just knew I was going to have to go to Africa. That was not where I wanted to go! So I simply ignored Him. Or at least I tried to. Have you ever tried to ignore God? He is not easy to ignore.

It seemed like every time I was in the bathtub, He wanted to talk about this missionary thing. I don't know why He chose the bathtub, other than the fact that it was a quiet place and I could hear Him better. I did my best to ignore Him for eight years, and then one fateful night at the First Baptist Church of Bangs, things finally came to a head.

Charlie and I had been married a few months. We didn't have a very long courtship–only four months elapsed from the time I said, "Hello, Charlie, my name is Pat Free," until I said, "I do" at the altar. My daddy had known Charlie for six years and worked with him at the Golden Hour Restaurant before Charlie went into the service. I had met Charlie's parents once, but I had never met Charlie during those years.

I became acquainted with Charlie's sister, Janice, through some mutual friends. We visited over the phone, and Janice invited me to spend the weekend at her house. We

Charlie and I had a very short engagement, but at least it was long enough for us to have an engagement portrait made! This picture is especially meaningful to me because our wedding album was lost during one of our many moves.

had several things planned for the weekend. When she picked me up that Friday evening, her brother, who had just finished a three year term in the Army, came with her. Janice and I never did get around to doing the things that we had planned, because I spent all of my time that weekend with her brother. Although we have done many things together in the last 48 years, she never has quite forgiven me for ruining that weekend. I bet if you ask her, though, she is quite thrilled that we are sisters-in-law.

Before Charlie and I were married, he was never interested

in going to church with me, though I invited him on several occasions. The month before we married, I decided to take a different approach. I invited him to go to the movies, which sounded like a safe place to him. I neglected to tell him that it was a Christian movie, *Time to Run*, produced by the Billy Graham Evangelistic Association. As we sat on the back row in the theater and watched the movie, God was in the process of totally changing our lives.

As Charlie watched the movie, God made him aware that his life was going in the wrong direction. He believed in God, but he knew that his heart did not belong to Jesus. As the film ended, several pastors stood at the front of the theater to receive those that wanted to come to Jesus for salvation. Tears began to roll down Charlie's cheeks. I don't know what I had expected to happen that night, but this was way beyond anything that I could have hoped for. Charlie left his seat and almost ran to the front, where a short, bald preacher led him to Christ. We walked out of the Bowie Theater in Brownwood, Texas that night with our lives changed forever.

After Charlie and I married on July 2, 1966, we lived in a small apartment in his hometown of Brownwood, Texas, for about six months. When we found the little apartment I was so thrilled. There is just something wonderful about your first home. When we were looking for this

This newspaper photo is the only wedding picture we have. As fuzzy as it is, you can see my beautiful champagne brocade wedding dress, handmade by my stepmother's sister, Jeri Michalk. I kept the dress through many moves, and finally gave it to my daughter-in-law, Karri Anne, for safekeeping.

first apartment, in my excitement it didn't occur to me to check for drawers in the kitchen cabinets. Moving day came, and of course, the first place a woman wants to start unpacking is in her kitchen. I got out the silverware, cup towels and potholders, but to my great surprise there was not a drawer in that kitchen. The only saving grace was the pantry. One whole shelf in the pantry held everything that should have been in the cabinet drawers. It didn't matter, though . . . it was our first home.

We also didn't have a washer and dryer, but a laundromat was right across the street. Since we didn't have much money, I decided I would wash our clothes and linens in the bathtub. I figured Charlie would not want me to do that, so I was pretty discreet about how I did it. I waited until he left for work and then I got all the dirty clothes out and got busy. I always made sure that I was finished and had left no traces by the time he came home in the afternoon.

I had been doing laundry in the bathtub for about three weeks when Charlie decided to surprise me and come home early. I shall never forget the look on his face as he stepped into the bathroom and saw me bent over the bathtub washing his blue jeans. I didn't know at the time if he wanted to get mad or cry. Needless to say, after that I spent my laundry days at the laundromat.

After living in our apartment for about six months, we moved about nine miles to a little rental house in my hometown of Bangs. (This time I made sure to check out the kitchen a little closer!) We continued going to church in Brownwood, although one particular Sunday night we decided to go to a service in Bangs. I am sure we had a reason for doing that, but in the Spiritual realm, it was simply one of those Divine Appointments. God had made an appointment with me, and this time we would talk.

Much to my surprise, the young man who was preaching that night was a former schoolmate of mine. He wasn't more than eighteen or nineteen years old and it was his first sermon. That sounds pretty harmless, but I walked out of that building knowing nothing would ever be the same in my life. God spoke to me through the young man's sermon, and I knew I could ignore Him no longer.

Charlie had not been raised in the Church, so as a brand new Christian, this was all new to him. I did not have a clue how I was going to tell him about God's call on my life. Now you have to remember, I still thought I would need to go to Africa to be a missionary. Moving to Bangs was one thing, but I was pretty sure Charlie didn't want to move to Africa. For a Brownwood boy, even Bangs was a stretch.

We went straight home after church without saying a single word. Charlie wasn't really sure what was going on. After we got home, I went straight to the bathroom (that place where God likes to talk), and Charlie went to the kitchen to make popcorn. In that bathroom I told God I would go to Africa if that was what He wanted. I remember asking Him what I would do with Charlie. Satan had me convinced that Charlie would leave me. But I knew I couldn't tell God "no" any longer. I was a new bride, and I was sure that my marriage would soon end.

I was in the bathroom for only thirty minutes when Charlie came in to check on me. As a new husband, he figured he had done something to upset me. Boy, did he have a surprise waiting for him behind that door. He walked in wanting to know what was going on. For the next hour I told him all about my call, from the time I was thirteen to the present. Then, through my tears, I asked him, "But what am I going to do with you?" That sounds so funny to me now after all these years, but believe me, it was anything but funny at that moment.

The most wonderful words came out of Charlie's mouth. He said, "Don't you think God might be calling me too?" That had never once occurred to me!

I dried my tears, and though it was midnight, we got into our Chevy and drove to Brownwood to see our pastor,

Neal Sheppard. We talked, cried and prayed. That night both of us gave our lives in full service to God, even if it meant Africa. Eight years after first hearing God's call to full-time ministry, it was now the *appointed time* to begin preparations. We didn't waste any time getting started. *Suddenly*, we were to answer His call and get ready for what God had in store for our lives.

In the following years, we traveled to a lot of places and did many things with God, but Africa hasn't been one of them—at least not yet! Don't think for one minute it hasn't been just as challenging. In fact, every time I get in the bathtub, I wonder what new and exciting things God will say.

Chapter Four

Answering the Call

God will make this happen, for he who calls you is faithful.

I Thessalonians 5:24 (New Living Translation)

In the fall of 1966, Charlie and I enrolled in Howard Payne College, a Baptist college in Brownwood, where we both majored in Religious Education. Within a year Charlie was pastoring his first church in Brownwood, while also holding down two other jobs and going to school. On August 16, 1967, our son Daman was born. I thought for awhile that I was going to deliver that baby all alone. Charlie happened to choose the day of Daman's birth to pick pears in some faraway orchard. In his defense, if he had known that Daman would choose that day to be born, Charlie would have stayed closer to home.

When I could wait no longer, some of our neighbors in the Ministerial Apartments loaded me into a car and drove me to the hospital. Four hours later, Charlie finally came home. My friends' husbands told Charlie of my whereabouts, but he laughed and ignored them. This group of men had a history of playing practical jokes, and Charlie assumed he was the recipient of another joke. When Charlie finally realized I was truly in labor and it was not a joke, he made it to the hospital in record time. Actually, he could have gone back to the orchard and picked another load of pears because Daman decided to drag out his arrival for twenty-six hours.

Because of my polio, the doctors had some concern about my ability to deliver Daman normally. After twenty-six hours of labor, they were even more concerned. Charlie found a quiet place to be alone and to cry out to God, asking for the ordeal to end and for us to be safe. Soon after, we had a healthy baby boy. It never really occurred to me that everything wouldn't be just fine.

We were off to a whirlwind start. Between July 2, 1966 and August 16, 1967, we had married, answered God's call, enrolled in Howard Payne College and delivered our first child. It only took us thirteen months and fourteen days to get it all accomplished!

Almost immediately, we tried to go to the mission field through the Southern Baptist mission program. However, we soon found out that it was not going to happen. My childhood polio left me in braces and crutches, and I simply could not pass the physical. We were disappointed, but it did not keep us from the ministry. For the next eighteen years, we pastored Southern Baptist Churches in Texas and New Mexico. I assumed that God didn't really intend for me to go to the mission field after all. He simply wanted me to be a preacher's wife, so I laid it all aside. Actually, I was quite happy to do it; I didn't have to think about Africa anymore!

Our lives were quite normal for the next several years—as normal as they can be in a Baptist parsonage. Our second son, Tommy, was born almost three years after our Daman. His arrival didn't take quite so long; he was anxious to get here and get started. He began letting me know that he wanted out at 7 a.m. on July 7, 1970 and by 10 a.m. he had pushed the door wide open. This time Charlie was right there and ready when I said, "Let's go."

Charlie and I both were much more relaxed when Tommy made his entrance. Charlie sat outside the door of the delivery room reading the newspaper. He was gearing up for a long wait. He never dreamed that we could have a child in three hours, and neither did I. After only three hard pains, I heard the doctor say, "Here he comes." I couldn't believe what I was hearing.

I have often thought that Tommy and I could have handled that one by ourselves and saved the cost of the hospital.

I asked Charlie years later if he was sorry that we didn't have four boys instead of two. He quickly replied, "No." "Why not?" I asked. "Because then we would have four old pickups sitting out front instead of two," he answered.

It never once occurred to me that I would not be able to have children because of my polio, but it did to my Aunt Mary, Daddy's sister. From the time that I was a young child, Aunt Mary prayed that I would be able to deal with the disappointment of not having children. When we announced that Daman was on the way, it surprised quite a few family members who had prayed long and hard for me. Tommy came along almost three years later.

I had received Jesus as my Savior when I was eight years old, but shortly after Charlie and I married and we had given our lives in service to God fulltime, I began to have doubts about my salvation. For twelve years I struggled. Some days there would be peace, and I would know that Jesus was mine and I was His, and there were other days I could hardly hold my head up and all I wanted to do was cry. I pretty much kept a happy face to the world, though. I needed to. I was the preacher's wife, remember?

The harder I tried to be good enough, the worse my doubts became. There is a reason for that. God could not allow me to rest and find peace in my good works. My good works could not save me. I knew that. If you had asked me, I would have given you the right answer. And yet, without knowing it, it was the very thing that I was trying to do.

During those twelve years, I can't even begin to tell you how many times I got down on my knees and asked God to save me. You need to understand that I was not trying to get saved over and over–I personally do not believe in that–I was simply trying to discover if I had been saved in the first place. I would get up feeling somewhat better, but within a few days all my doubts would return.

I remember once crying myself to sleep because I couldn't find peace. I woke up in the middle of the night, sat straight up in the bed and began to quote the Scripture; *Greater is He* (Jesus) *that is in you* (Pat) *than he* (Satan) *who is in the world.* You would think that would have settled the issue of my salvation. God was certainly trying to do His part. It helped for a couple of days, and then I was right back where I had started. It is hard to get saved when you are *already* saved.

God and I won that battle with Satan at 7:30 pm on August 8, 1978, while we were pastoring Deming First Baptist Church. Evangelist Mickey Bonner was holding revival services in our Church. Before the service started that night, I told God I couldn't go on like that any longer. I had to know whether I was saved or lost. I asked Him to make it really clear to me and I would take the necessary steps no matter what—preacher's wife or no preacher's wife.

When Brother Bonner stepped up to the pulpit to preach, he began by saying something that I will never forget as long as I live: *"God has changed my message tonight. I rarely ever preach on salvation, but tonight the Lord has led me to do so. My ministry has been in the area of deliverance and to encourage the Body of Christ, but I really sense the Lord saying that there are thirty to fifty percent of you sitting out there that Satan has lied to causing you to doubt your salvation."*

Brother Bonner didn't have a clue that I was one of those people. I had not said a word to him prior to the service.

The only person who ever knew what I was going through was Charlie, and he didn't really know the full extent of my doubt.

I couldn't tell you another thing Brother Bonner said that night, because the moment he spoke those words, I could physically feel the deception leave me. I was free from Satan's lie. I wanted to stand up and shout! His words were life and truth to me, exactly what my heart needed to hear. I left the service that night knowing that God had heard and answered my prayer.

Somewhere along the way I had opened a door; it gave Satan a foothold to come in and place seeds of doubt in my heart about God's acceptance of me. Satan loves to cause us to doubt God, whether it is for our salvation or our healing or for our destiny, and I had played right into his hand. Satan told me that I wasn't good enough to be saved. He still tells me that, only now I am smart enough to agree with him. I am not good enough, but God never expected me to be good enough. That is why He sent Jesus, who is good enough for us both. I could never be good enough, no matter how hard I tried. If I could have done it on my own, then the death of Jesus was certainly a waste. I couldn't save myself, and I will tell you another little secret, I can't keep myself saved either. Let me declare to you right now, I need Jesus for everything. I love being totally dependent upon Jesus. That is freedom to me, and it certainly takes a lot of pressure off me. He is my Savior in every area of my life.

Being the preacher's wife was challenging at times, but it was a good life. We had wonderful opportunities to work with the Body of Christ, and the friendships we have made throughout the years are priceless. I wish time and space would allow me to tell you something about each church we pastored, but it won't. I will tell you this, though: God used each place to teach me something of value that I would one day need at the appointed time.

Chapter Five

Sitting At the Kitchen Table

For God's gifts and His call are irrevocable. [He never withdraws them when once they are given, and He does not change His mind about those to whom He gives His grace or to whom He sends His call.]

Romans 11:29 (Amplified Bible)

In the first chapter, I spoke about hearing God say "suddenly." A couple of days after He spoke, I sat our kitchen table reading my Bible and spending some time in prayer with the Lord. The next thing I knew I was in the middle of another *suddenly*. This time God said, "I am getting Charlie and you ready for a *special ministry."* Those were pretty exciting words to me. I immediately began to wonder what God meant by *special ministry.*

We had already been down the missionary road, so I knew that was out of the question. It is *evangelism*! *God wants us to go into evangelism*! I settled that pretty quickly! So quickly that I pulled out the bottom drawer of our china cabinet, turned it upside down and wrote the date and what God had just said to me, and boldly wrote that Charlie was going to be an evangelist. Several years later I sold that china cabinet to a lady in Deming. I have often wondered if she ever turned that drawer upside down, and what she must have thought. Sometimes I can get a little ahead of God and myself!

The next day, I went to the church to speak to Brother Bonner about the impact that his sermon on Salvation had in my life. While I was talking to him, he said to me, "Pat, God is getting Charlie and you ready for an end-time ministry, and if Satan can stop it through you he will." The first part I was pretty excited about, but I wasn't too sure about the second. It didn't make a lot of sense to me. The last thing on earth I wanted to do was to stop Charlie from a special, end-time ministry. It would be years before I would understand how Satan could possibly use me to stop such a thing.

As I walked out of the office with Brother Bonner that day, a precious Christian lady in our church, Gladys Eichoff, came up to me. Gladys was in her 80s at the time and strong in the Lord, and she had something really important to tell me. We walked over to a corner in the fellowship hall, and she said, "Pat, God has spoken to me like this only one other time in my whole life. He has shown me that He is getting Charlie and you ready for a *special ministry." A special ministry*—the very words that God had used with me, just the day before. In less than twenty-four hours God had spoken to me and to two others concerning a *special, end-time ministry.*

Brother Bonner has since gone on to be with the Lord, but before he left, God used him mightily on more than one occasion to help set the course of my destiny. Brother Bonner is one of the people that I will want to see pretty soon after I get to heaven. Most likely he already knows how God used him in my life. I just want to tell him "thank you" one more time.

I shared very little with Charlie about what Brother Bonner and Gladys had said. I knew when God got ready to move in Charlie's life concerning all of this, He would make it known to him. I didn't want to get in the way of God's timing, and besides, I knew Charlie would need to hear it from God rather than from me. What I did do was pray. I would rather have prayed just a few months and seen it all materialize, but I thank God it didn't. First, we were not mature enough spiritually for what God was going to require of us. Secondly, our whole lives would have to be turned upside down first.

I prayed for twenty-two years before I saw that *special, end-time ministry* realized. There was rarely a day in twenty-two years that I didn't talk to God about it. I never grew weary discussing it with Him. With each passing year the vision grew stronger and stronger and I knew that I would see it come to pass.

People have asked me how I knew that it was God speaking to me. I wish I could explain but I am not sure there are words to describe it. I just knew it was His voice. It is a little like knowing my sons' voices. Those two boys could be in a crowd of thousands, and if either one grabbed a microphone and called my name, I would immediately recognize his voice over everybody else's in the crowd. I *know* them. Jesus said in His word, *"My sheep that are My own hear and are listening to My voice; and I know them, and they follow Me"* (*John 10:27*, Amplified Bible).

We pastored another five years in New Mexico, until there was nothing left in us that wanted to continue. We were tired and disillusioned, not with God, but with ministry as we had known it. We actually didn't know what was going on. It was hard to even put it into words. About all we knew was that God wanted us out of the pastoral ministry. That wasn't the easiest decision we had ever made. Pastoring was all we had known for eighteen and a half years. I remember feeling like we had stepped out on God. At times I felt sick to my stomach about it all, yet other times there was complete peace.

Where was the *special, end-time ministry* going to fit in now? We had "left" the ministry! I didn't know where it was going to fit, but I knew that it was going to fit somewhere, because I had a promise from God that I wasn't about to throw away.

We sold our house in 1983, packed up our belongings and moved back to Texas. Charlie went to work with one of his cousins in Breckenridge, Texas, laying pipe for a few months. Then, out of nowhere, a strange door opened for us. I would have never guessed in a million years what we were about to do. We were about to step into an *appointed time.*

Chapter Six

A Strange Turn of Events

But thanks be to God, Who in Christ always leads us in triumph [as trophies of Christ's victory] and through us spreads and makes evident the fragrance of the knowledge of God everywhere.

2 Corinthians 2:14 (Amplified Bible)

"*You are going to do what*?" That was my stunned response when Charlie came home one day and told me that he was going to apply for the city marshal's job in Cross Plains, Texas. I looked at him and wondered what made him come up with that idea. So, I asked him. He told me he wasn't really sure, but he felt like it was something that he would enjoy doing. He filled out the application form and we prayed. Within the week, the city fathers called and offered Charlie the job without his having one ounce of experience.

We packed up our belongings, and in 1984 we moved once

again, this time to Cross Plains. It must have looked like our train had derailed, and I know people were worried about us. After all, we had been pastor and family for eighteen and a half years and now we had left full-time ministry and were going into law enforcement! I had heard of men going from law enforcement into the pastorate, but never the other way around. This was certainly a strange turn of events. Nothing was turning out like I thought it would. We seemed to be going in the opposite direction of a *special, end-time ministry*, but nothing in me wanted to let go of that promise. Even though I could not see one shred of evidence, I continued to lift that promise to God and thank Him for it.

We moved into a little rental house in the middle of Johnson Trucking's truck yard. The business was on one side and a junkyard was on the other. Because Charlie had not a single day of police training, Cross Plains enrolled him in the Police Academy in Abilene. He went to school during the day and was on duty as city marshal at night.

We made a whopping $1,300 a month. If manna had not come from heaven, we could not have made it. Thanks to a lady who worked at the Town & Country Store, we had lots of leftover chicken and burritos. She gave us all the leftovers at the end of each day rather than dumping them in the trash as she was supposed to. We weren't too proud to take them either, because by now we had Charlie's little cousin, Lisa, living with us. We were five!

I know living next to a junkyard does not sound pretty, but it wasn't as bad as it sounds. Our side and back yards were filled with oak trees, twenty-eight to be exact. They were absolutely gorgeous.

Every morning I got Charlie off to the academy in Abilene, our boys and Lisa off to school, and then I sat down outside under the shelter of the twenty-eight oak trees. I stayed there for an hour and a half to two hours talking things over with the Lord. Just like those oak trees, His presence surrounded me.

For the first time in my adult life, I didn't have anything to offer to God but myself. Before I had been the preacher's wife, taught Sunday school, sang in the church choir, led the ladies Bible study, conducted children's church, etc., etc., etc. All those things that I had done for God were gone. I wasn't really sure how He would feel about me now. It didn't take Him long to tell me though. I was telling Him all about it one day in my little prayer closet of oak trees, feeling pretty useless, when He said, "All I want is *you*!"

A floodgate of tears poured out of me for a long time that day. For the first time in my life, I knew that I was *totally* accepted by God with nothing to offer but myself. Until then I had lived in a performance mode, and I am still not sure why. I grew up with a lot of acceptance. Even though my parents were divorced and I spent part of my childhood living away from my mother, I don't ever remember feeling unloved. In 1957, my daddy moved my younger brother Dan and me to Houston, and all three of us lived with his mother. Two years later, Daddy married our pastor's daughter, Jo Ann Collier Pratt. She already had two little boys in diapers, Steve and Monty, and then our little brother, Dale, came along. God has always surrounded me with loving family and friends.

Charlie and I lived in Cross Plains for one year. It still remains at the top of my list as a place of spiritual growth. At the end of that year, it was time to pack those boxes once again and unpack them in a small west Texas town called Snyder.

We settled into Snyder as comfortably as a hand in an old glove, and enjoyed living there for the next fifteen years. Charlie went to work for the Scurry County Sheriff's Department as a deputy sheriff, and I went to work at First United Methodist Church as their secretary, where I remained for the next eleven and a half years. This would not be our church home, but many of the people in the church became very special to us.

After two years of visiting different churches, we found our church home, Word is Life, and became a part of the Christian community. We had many wonderful experiences through the years in which we grew in our faith. We also became a part of the Walk to Emmaus, a 72-hour non-denominational spiritual retreat, and had the privilege of getting to know other Christian brothers and sisters in churches that otherwise we might never have known.

One morning in 1997, out of the clear blue, God began to speak to me about the need for a piano in our living room. At first I thought that was a little strange since I didn't play the piano and actually had no desire to learn, but I knew that prompting was coming from God, so I began to actively pray about a piano for our living room. One thing that God made clear to me was that I was not to go out searching for a piano. I was to only talk to Him about it. The prayer had originated with Him, and God wanted it to remain with Him. He didn't want me trying to make it happen, which I could have done easily enough, since there were a lot of secondhand pianos for sale. I didn't know it at the time, but God was about to teach me a major life lesson, one that I would draw on many times in the future.

For approximately six months, I reminded God from time to time that He said I needed a piano in the living room.

The spot where it would sit was all picked out. I had no doubt that it was coming!

Early one Saturday morning, the phone rang. It was Dorothy Petersen, a friend, but we seldom saw each other and rarely talked on the phone. I remember thinking that she must need something or else she wouldn't be calling. She knew nothing about God's promise of a piano. I asked Dorothy what she was up to. She told me that she was trying to rearrange one of her rooms so her computer would fit better. She said that there was too much clutter, and that she had to get rid of some stuff.

I began to laugh out loud when I heard her next words, "I have this piano in here, and I don't know what to do with it." I asked Dorothy if she wanted to sell her piano. She said, "Well, I sure need to get rid of it, since I don't have any place for it." When I asked her how much she wanted for it, she replied, "I really think I am just supposed to give it to you." I said, "I think you are, too, Dorothy."

After months of praying, it was God's *appointed time* for me to get a piano. *Suddenly* His promise was to be fulfilled. I didn't let any grass grow under my feet. I quickly rounded up four men to help Charlie pick up the piano and placed it in the living room in the designated spot. After the guys left, I sat down at the dining room table next to the piano. There is just something very exciting about knowing that you have heard God correctly. I sat there for a time thanking God for the piano.

After a little bit, God begin to show me what the piano was all about. Here is what He spoke to my heart that day: *"Do you see with what ease that piano came? This is how I want you to receive everything from My hand. You didn't have to beg, or plead, or cry for this piano. You didn't have to feel that you weren't good enough, or that you were not worthy enough to have this piano in your living room. You didn't have to go out searching for a piano. All you did was to remind Me of what I had said. You simply received what I told you that I wanted you to have. Now, every time Satan tries to tell you that you are not worthy of something that I want you to have, bring him over here and show him this piano!"*

I believe this is one of the most important lessons that God has ever taught me. I cannot tell you how many times I have drawn upon this principle. When God speaks to me about something that He wants, I am learning to be still, believe Him, and let Him do it. I am not talking about being passive. Faith is very active! Every day I go before God and talk to Him about the things I believe that He wants me to have and the things that He wants me to do with my life.

He knows that I am coming! I have been coming to Him

in faith for one thing or another for most of my life. He constantly checks up on me and asks me what I am believing Him for. He has never said I am asking for too much. From time to time He reminds me to keep my faith in Him and not in man. I am sure the reason that He does that is because *with men it is impossible, but with God all things are possible.* (*Matthew 19:26,* Holman Christian Standard Bible).

If you are not careful, it is easy to find yourself looking to men for answers rather than God. God has always used people to bless other people and sometimes to bring about His answers, but He wants our focus to be on Him. He has some impossible things to give us that mere man, with all of his money and abilities, cannot deliver.

I never did learn to play that piano. That was not God's intention in the first place, and even though that piano is long gone from my possession, I still get a lot of use out of it. Every time Satan tells me that I am not going to receive God's promises, or that God has surely forgotten me because the answer has been too long in coming, or that my Christian life is not good enough to deserve the impossible from God, I am happy to remind him of the Saturday morning when I stood in my living room and watched God honor His word to me.

Chapter Seven

Change Is Coming!

"Yes," Jesus replied, "and I assure you that everyone who has given up house or brothers or sisters or mother or father or children or property, for my sake and for the Good News, will receive now in return a hundred times as many houses, brothers, sisters, mothers, children, and property—along with persecution. And in the world to come that person will have eternal life.

Mark 10:29-30 (New Living Translation)

As comfortable as we were in Snyder, I knew that God had more in store for us. Almost daily I continued to pray and believe that God's promise of a *special, end-time ministry* was ours. I knew there was an *appointed time* and that it required a wait. From the time that God gave that word to me in 1978, I never doubted it. The journey had definitely taken some strange turns and going from the pulpit to the patrol car was one of them. Even that would make perfect sense one day.

In 1998 our son and daughter-in-law, Tommy and Holly, attended Trinity Fellowship Church in San Angelo, Texas under the leadership of Billy Simmons and Randy Levens. One Sunday morning they had a special guest speaker. During the ministry time, the speaker asked Tommy and Holly to stand, and he began to prophecy over them. It was a lengthy prophecy, but the words at the end impacted me greatly: *"Now when the full will of God is accomplished and perfected, the Lord says, do not in that day and in that time get so locked into only one working of ministry, one idea, one concept of ministry that you fail to see the larger call that I am calling you to. For I may send you to places in time, but I will also have you building for Me a place, a place that I can send people that are hurting, wounded, and broken. And I will make of you restorers, restorers of people, restorers of those that are wounded, beaten, those that have been cast down low, and you will be strengthened of God to speak into their lives and teach them deeper things, even to pray prayers of deliverance and healing over them. You will be effective in all that you do, says the Lord."*

The prophecy was recorded, and when I heard it replayed, I knew the words were for Charlie and me. The words could have been for Tommy and Holly as well, because a prophecy is often for more than one person.

At this point in our lives, we had no intention of building anything. I still knew the words were meant for us. I cannot tell you how many times I read and prayed over those words in the coming years, asking God to show us what He meant by them. God had every intention of doing just that, but it would be in His time. We would not find out for another six years.

One morning in early 1999, I received a phone call from Marsha Sanders, a woman who attended our church. I did not know Marsha very well at that time, so her early morning phone call was unexpected. She said, "Sister Pat, I had a dream about you and Brother Charlie last night. I saw your house on a hill. Charlie was driving a turquoise pickup, and I was with him."

I questioned her about her dream, but she told me that was all she remembered. As we hung up, I thought, "I don't want a house on the hill. I want Mrs. Merritt's house right next door to me." I had my eye on Mrs. Merritt's house for quite awhile; I had looked at it a couple of times and was ready to make an offer. I even had Charlie convinced that it would be the perfect house for us. I didn't give Marsha's dream much thought because it didn't fit into my plans. But then again, God had His own plans and in due time, He would reveal them to us.

Charlie worked for the Scurry County Sheriff's Department for almost twelve years before he left to become the Justice of the Peace of Scurry County. He was in his fifth year as Justice of the Peace, with three years left on his second term, when I began to see a growing unrest in him. I had seen that look before, and I recognized it for what it was–God was making changes again!

About four months later, Charlie went on a mission trip to Guatemala, Central America, with our pastor, Tony Wofford, and some others from our church. It was a simple mission trip to build a house for a lady who was very much in need. He had a great time as he had on other mission trips in the past. That was all there was to it, he thought.

One weekend after Charlie returned from Guatemala, we drove to San Angelo to visit our two sons and their families. We went to church together and then out to eat. Charlie was pretty antsy, more than usual. To say the least, he wasn't himself. He picked up our little ten-month-old granddaughter, Addie, and went outside. After Charlie left the table, our sons asked, "What is wrong with Dad?" I told them that I wasn't sure, but I felt like they needed to get ready for some change. When I said that, Tommy, our son, and Karri Anne, Daman's wife, said in unison, "So when are you moving to Guatemala?" I looked at them, thinking "you have got to be kidding me!" The idea had not crossed my mind.

After lunch the following Sunday, I stretched out to rest and read for a while when God *suddenly* had a word for me. He said, *"Change is coming."* I remember laying my book down, because I didn't want to miss a word that He had to say. But that was it—change is coming! I was very aware that He didn't mean sometime in the future. He meant right now . . . gear up and hang on to your hat!

Three days later, Charlie came home for lunch as usual. I worked for the Scurry County District Clerk's Office and had arrived home before him to prepare lunch. He stepped into the kitchen and stood by the door without saying anything. When he finally spoke, his words forever changed our lives: "Well, mama, are you ready to go to Guatemala?"

When Charlie posed that question, he just knew the fight would be on. We had not really talked about our *special, end-time ministry* in all the years since 1978, only little snippets of conversation every so often. He was sure I couldn't bear leaving our grandchildren. Our first grandson, Kylan, was only eleven years old, Addie had just been born ten months before, and Holly and Tommy were expecting their first child, Harrison, in a little over three months.

He was shocked when I said to him, "As a matter of fact, I am ready." I was as calm as I had ever been in my life. God had been preparing me for this moment since that fateful day, August 8, 1978, when He said, *"I am getting Charlie and you ready for a special ministry."*

We began to make plans to leave for Guatemala, but before God would allow us to go, He and Charlie had to get something straight. Because Charlie had grown up in a family living paycheck to paycheck, he was determined that his family would always have financial security. He wanted health insurance, retirement funds, and something in the bank to fall back on. Now God was asking him to give up everything.

One night, Charlie lay awake in the early morning hours. He got up, went into our living room and began to pour his heart out to God about his concerns about retirement, hospitalization, and how we were going to live without income. He could see no answers. With a heavy heart, he said, "God, what about my benefits?" God very quickly responded, *"Charlie, what about My benefits?"* That brief answer settled it for Charlie. He got up from his chair with peace in his heart and the knowledge that if God had called us, He would provide for us. For the first time in our lives, God truly became our provider.

Within four months, we sold or gave away everything we owned, quit our jobs, and with many tears, told our family and friends good-bye. After twenty two years of praying and waiting, God finally gave us the go-ahead with these words, *"I want you to go like Abraham went, and as you go, I will tell you what you are to do, but not before."* It was the *appointed time,* and *suddenly* His words were being fulfilled.

As we drove away from Tommy and Holly's home on February 15, 2000, Tommy's parting words were, "Now, Dad, don't go down there and get a poverty mentality." I always thought Tommy made that statement because he knew it would be hard for Charlie to keep anything of value while seeing the poverty of the people around him. Tommy knew his dad's heart.

In the days and years ahead, we would see a faithful God provide for us, His children, in ways we would never have imagined. God has always seen to it that we have had more than enough to do the things that He has called us to do. We began our journey that day with many tears, but with grateful hearts to be finally realizing the twenty-two-year-old promise from God—*"I am getting you ready for a special, end-time ministry."*

People are surprised when we tell them we drove to Guatemala from Texas. We did not know one word of Spanish, so when Charlie stopped to buy gas, he would raise his hand up and keep it going higher. The station attendants knew right away that he wanted the tank filled to the top. I never will forget the first time we filled up in Mexico. I was in the front seat; suddenly the car starting rocking back and forth. My heart went to my toes. I was sure the attendants were out to harm us, but they were just trying to get more gas into the vehicle by rocking it back and forth. That was the first of many exciting experiences as we traveled through Mexico and Guatemala.

On the third day of our five-and-a-half day journey, we were driving down a dirt road out in the middle of nowhere with no houses in sight, when all of a sudden we came upon a little shack that seemed to be a military checkpoint. Believe me, we did not want to stop, but we knew that it would be wise to do so. Two soldiers came to the car and asked Charlie to get out of the vehicle, but they allowed me to remain inside.

Our four-wheel-drive Trooper was loaded with all our earthly possessions. One of the men started going through our things in the back, while another opened the side door and began his search. To Charlie's dismay, a soldier took one of Charlie's ball caps and put it on his own head without asking permission. This didn't set well with Charlie! Charlie would give you the shirt off of his back, if he thought you needed it. But, don't expect him to stand there and let someone steal from him—not on your life.

You need to understand this man had a gun, as did the other three men standing around that checkpoint, and let's not forget another man was going through our belongings in the back seat. Charlie reached out and snatched his cap off the soldier's head. I thought, "Charlie, give him the stupid cap, for heaven's sake! They all have guns!" But God is faithful! He came through for us that day.

I still wear leg braces from my childhood polio. Earlier that warm Mexican afternoon, I decided to pull off the one brace I was wearing at the time and put it in the back seat. About the same time that Charlie pulled the cap from the soldier's head, the officer checking the inside of our vehicle lifted up my brace. It shocked him so much that he threw it back down and yelled to the others to let us go. That is the only time in my life that I have ever been thankful for braces. The Scripture is true, *"God works in mysterious ways."*

After almost six days, we finally arrived in Guatemala. Our first stop was Lake Atitlan, Panajachel, where we spent a week with Don Taylor. Don and his wife, Marlene, helped run Buenas Nuevas Retreat Center. Don and Marlene are the parents of Julie Long, whom we had known in Snyder. The night before we closed the doors to our house and left Snyder, we received a phone call from Julie. She had felt strongly that God wanted us to call her dad and make arrangements to stay with him for a few days.

At her urging, we called Don, introduced ourselves and told him our plans. He immediately said, "Come and stay with me for a few days. You are going to be tired by the time you get here. You will need to rest." He was so right! By the time we arrived at his gate, we were exhausted physically and emotionally. Charlie was sick from contaminated food and two days later, I became sick as well. We were so glad to be there in a nice, clean, safe environment. It was also the first time that we were able to call our sons and daughters-in-law since we had started our trip. We all needed to hear from each other at that point.

Less than two days later, the big gates to the property opened wide for more weary travelers, Doane and Mellisa Brueckner from Brenham, Texas. They, too, were on a God journey and they had many questions as well. Along with Don, we spent the days together. We had some wonderful conversations, each of us sharing what God was doing in our lives. We were all aware that God had brought us together. It was good and it was needed.

Don could not have done a better job caring for us that week even though Marlene was visiting in the U.S. Don nursed us back to health, fed us, introduced us around, and got us enrolled in the Christian Spanish Academy in Antigua, Guatemala. We moved in with a Guatemalan family and lived and breathed Spanish for the next two weeks.

One afternoon, we received a phone call from our friend Stanley Clark from Snyder. Stanley was coming to Guatemala for a few days and wanted to meet us in Antigua for coffee. We were pretty excited at the thought of seeing someone from back home. Stanley had mentioned that he needed to take care of some business in Guatemala, and was bringing his mom, Carla, with him. Whatever the reason, we were just ready to see friends!

We met the Clarks in Antigua the next day and sat around a pastry shop table with our pie and coffee, telling them our stories about our trip through Mexico and Guatemala. We laughed a lot that day. It was a wonderful time and one that we needed very badly. Even though we had left the States only three weeks earlier, it felt like three months. We had left sons, daughters-in-law and grandchildren, and our hearts were raw.

Several times, Stanley invited us to join them in San Cristóbal in Alta Vera Paz, where they were staying for the weekend. Each time we thanked him and declined the offer, explaining that we were loaded down with Spanish homework. Studying a new language was enough of a challenge for Charlie and me at our age, let alone a rough six-hour trip to San Cristóbal with very little help from road signs and barely any ability to ask for directions.

After a couple of delightful hours, it was time for Stanley and Carla to get on the road. They had a long journey ahead of them and it was getting late. Stanley asked one more time if we would reconsider his invitation to come up for the weekend. We gave him the same answer as we had the other four times, "Thank you, but we just can't," and said our goodbyes.

As Stanley walked away, Charlie and I looked at each other and instantly knew we needed to accept Stanley's invitation. We had been asking God to show us what we were to do in Guatemala. Could Stanley's insistence be a part of God's answer?

Charlie caught up with Stanley, told him that we would leave as soon as our classes were over on Friday, and got directions. Oh, what a *suddenly* awaited us in San Cristóbal.

Chapter Eight

Wasting No Time

Do not fret or have any anxiety about anything, but in every circumstance and in everything, by prayer and petition (definite requests), with thanksgiving, continue to make your wants known to God.

Philippians 4:6 (Amplified Bible)

We arrived in San Cristóbal just before dark. Even though it had been a wild ride, the country was breathtaking. It also felt good to get away from our Spanish books. We were in our fifties trying to learn another language, and that alone can take a lot out of you. Let me suggest if you have the slightest inkling you might need to speak another language some day, start learning it right now while all of your brain cells are still functioning.

Early the next morning, Stanley took Charlie to meet some local people, They first stopped to see Mike and LaTonya Lewis, missionaries in Guatemala for many years who had a church and a private Christian school. They were in need of English teachers and help in general, and had been praying that God would send them someone.

At one point, Mike, LaTonya, Stanley and Charlie were standing on the front porch, and Mike's mind was going in a thousand directions. As he told us later, he asked the Lord, "What am I supposed to do with this man?"

God answered, "Haven't you been praying for help?" "Yes," Mike said. "Well, I have put him on your porch, what more do you want Me to do?"

When they got back into the car, Charlie asked Stanley, "What just happened back there?" Stanley laughed and said; "I think Mike just offered you a job, if you want it!"

Charlie and Stanley were home by 11:00 a.m. I was getting dressed and fixing my face when Charlie stuck his head through the bathroom door and said, "Hurry up and get ready. We are having lunch with some missionaries. I think this is where we are meant to be." I said, "You are kidding. We just got here!"

I liked the Lewises immediately. We spent several hours talking about how we might help them in their ministry. But, where would we live? San Cristóbal didn't have many rental houses.

To tell you the truth, we were not quite ready to be alone in Guatemala. The Christian Spanish Academy in Antigua required that we live with a Guatemalan family that spoke only Spanish to us. After two weeks of that, we were ready for some English!

LaTonya said, "What about the room at the front of the school?" A family was living in it at the time, but they were to move that week. Charlie and I looked at it, and then we looked at each other. It was just a 10x20 room, but it had a bathroom and a bathtub! When I saw that bathtub, I knew this was going to be our home, and the size of the room made no difference to me. For the last three weeks, I had heated hot water in a coffee pot for sponge baths. I would heat hot water in the coffee pot for a few more months, but at least I could pour it into a bathtub now.

On Sunday morning, we left San Cristóbal to return briefly to Antigua. The next day, we loaded our few belongings, told our Guatemalan hosts good-bye, stopped by the school and paid our bill, and headed back to San Cristóbal. We fixed up the room and called it home for the next six and a half months. In one 10 x 20 space, we had room for our bed, stove, table and chairs, dishes, TV, computer, desk, rocking chair, hutch, microwave and clothes. Our refrigerator didn't fit, so it sat outside near the back door by the first grade classroom. We also had a small closet that we called our pantry because it held our dishes as well as our socks, shoes, and underwear.

We were thrilled to be there, and we felt that we finally had some direction. Actually, we had always had direction, but now God had chosen to share it with us. We left our family in the States, and God had seen fit to surround us with more family in Guatemala. Our new family consisted not only of the Lewises but other precious Guatemalans who helped us through our grieving period. They all played a major role in helping us become established in a new country and comfortable with the culture and language.

We never doubted for a minute that God had brought us to this place, but leaving our children and grandchildren was heart wrenching. There were many tears that first year, but God used the arms and hearts of these precious new friends to heal our hurting hearts. I remembered the words that Mickey Bonner spoke to me in the church office long ago: *"Pat, God is calling Charlie and you for an end-time ministry, and if Satan can stop it through you, he will."* When I told my family goodbye, I could see for the first time how Satan could have used me to stop this ministry. I am so very thankful that God had brought me to a place where His will for my life overruled anything and everyone else. God had assured me earlier if I would obey Him, my grandchildren would walk in a destiny that would not have been possible any other way.

Both of us taught English to the children in the school, and Charlie also helped Mike with some of the preaching in the church. We became Papaw Charlie and Mimi to the Lewis' five children and have remained that to this day.

After about six and a half months, a brand-new house became available in the village. I looked at that house and thought that God had it built just for us—it was perfect for us. You need to understand that new houses like that were not usually built in the indigenous village of San Cristóbal. Our new house had beautiful mahogany kitchen cabinets and even a laundry room. There was no bathtub, but Charlie and I were so thrilled to have a house that by now a bathtub didn't seem to matter that much. The great thing was we did have hot water!

We lived in that house for the next seven months. As great as everything was, we knew that our time with the people of San Cristóbal would not last forever. This was our starting place, but we knew that God had more in store for us. Though we had grown to love the people very much, and they will always hold a special place in our heart, God was ready to open new ministry doors for us. When they opened *suddenly*, some things made perfect sense.

Chapter Nine

The Man

Behold, I am the Lord, the God of all flesh;
is there anything too difficult for Me?
Jeremiah 32:27 (New American Standard)

Every year, the missionaries in Guatemala hold a three-day conference called Intermissions. Missionaries of every denomination come from all over the country, and it is a wonderful time of fellowship. In 2001, the conference was held in Antigua. Charlie and I considered going, but it was a six-hour trip down the winding mountain roads from San Cristóbal, and Charlie decided that he did not want to make the trip. He had already driven that road three times that month. It was settled. We would not go, even though a family in Antigua, Bob and Shirley Adams, offered us a place to stay free of charge.

A couple of weeks before Intermissions, we had our very first visitors from the States, Randy and Shauna Levens from San Angelo, Texas. We did not know the Levens very well, but we were glad to have them visit. Our son, Tommy, had often told us what a great teacher Randy was and wanted us to get to know him and his wife. From that first visit, we became good friends and have remained so to this day. The Levens have played a major role in His Appointed Time Ministries throughout the years.

After dinner one night, we were sitting around the table with Randy and Shauna when the phone rang. The family that offered us a place to stay during the Intermissions conference was calling for the fourth time. The previous three times, we had thanked Bob and Shirley for their offer but declined. The fourth time, Charlie's answer was the same, and he returned to the dinner table.

Because Randy heard the phone conversation, he asked Charlie what it was about. After Charlie explained, Randy told him, "Charlie, I don't usually say things like this, but I believe that you are to go to that conference and at that conference you will meet a *man* who will be very influential in your ministry in Guatemala." Because of our respect for Randy as a man of God, we called Bob and Shirley and accepted their offer. A few days later Randy and Shauna packed their bags to return home, and Charlie and I packed our bags and headed down the winding mountain road to attend the 2001 Intermissions conference to meet "**the**" man.

Throughout the conference, Charlie and I would look at each and ask, "Have you met **"the"** man yet?" Our answer was always, "No, I have met a lot of men, but I haven't met **"the"** man yet!" It really became quite comical, but nonetheless, we were on the lookout for **"the"** man.

The last day of the conference arrived, and it was time to eat lunch and go home. Charlie decided that we should not stay for the meal, that we needed to get on the road and head up the mountain before the traffic got too bad. We were going drive Chicky Donaldson, another missionary, to her home, and we told her we planned to skip lunch and grab something to eat on the way. Chicky responded, "Well, Charlie, we have to eat somewhere, so why don't we just eat here where the meal is already prepared?" Charlie agreed, "That is right. We will leave just as quickly as we can after lunch." I was quite thrilled. I always want to stay right to the very end. Besides, we still had not met **"the"** man.

During the conference we met Kendon and Wendy Wheeler, a missionary couple from the Lubbock, Texas area. After they learned about Charlie's background in law enforcement, they told us we should meet Randy and Marlene Green, who were also at the conference. Because we decided to stay for lunch, the Wheelers saved a place for us at their table and seated us right next to the Greens. Randy struck up a conversation with Charlie and told him about their ministry to the Guatemalan National Civil Police, and how they shared the Gospel of Jesus Christ by using defensive tactics training to open the doors.

After Randy finished sharing his story, he asked Charlie what he did. Charlie explained to him that we lived in San Cristóbal, teaching English in a Christian school and helping in the church. Randy then asked Charlie what he did before coming to the mission field. Charlie told him that he had pastored for eighteen and a half years, after which time, we felt God closed those door and opened new doors to work in law enforcement, where he worked for the Scurry County Sheriff's Department for eleven and a half years and then as the elected Justice of the Peace for five years.

When Charlie finished sharing his story, Randy looked at him and said, "Well, Charlie, my wife and I have been praying and fasting for the last month. We have been asking God to send us some help in this ministry. We have been very specific in our request to God. We have asked for three things—that God would send us a man that has been a pastor, a man that has been in law enforcement, and a man that is on the mission field right now." You could have heard a pin drop at that table. Charlie and I both looked at each other, and although we didn't say a word, we knew that we had just met **"the"** man.

We met Randy on the first of March. By the end of April, we unloaded all of our earthly belongings into a pretty

Even though Charlie does not work with the Police in Central America anymore, a part of his heart remains with that work. You will see him tearing up when he talks about those days of defensive training and the work he did to lead the officers to follow Jesus as their Savior.

little two-story house in San Lucas, Sacatepequez, just twenty minutes from Guatemala City. By this time we had "stuff" to unload. It's amazing what you can accumulate in thirteen months. Charlie worked with Randy Green, training the National Civil Police of Guatemala in defensive tactics and sharing the Gospel of Jesus Christ with the men and women in blue. For the first time since 1984, we fully understood God's leadership from the pulpit to the patrol car.

Charlie worked side by side with Randy for over a year, until the Lord called the Green family back to the States to begin a new work with police officers in other areas. For the next three-and-a-half years, Charlie continued the work all over Guatemala, El Salvador, and Honduras. Many doors were opened to Charlie, not because he had

Charlie has remained friends with many of the policemen he trained. We sit on the patio with the officers that come to visit, and serve them coffee and banana bread. It keeps the neighbors wondering when they see the uniformed officers drive up in their patrol cars.

been a pastor, but because he had been a deputy sheriff. His law enforcement years gave him credibility to speak into the lives of the police in Central America.

Years before, the Guatemalan police had been corrupt and abusive, and that led to laws limiting the police in what weapons they could use. If someone came after a cop with a club, for instance, the police officer could only use a club to apprehend him, not a gun. Officers weren't even allowed to carry a loaded gun. If someone fired at them, they had to stop and load their gun before they returned fire. Needless to say, many police officers were injured or killed on duty. The police were in sore need of

Charlie worked with police officers in Guatemala, El Salvador and Honduras for over four years. In this picture, he has just shared how they can receive Jesus as their Savior. The ones who want to receive Jesus have raised their hands.

self-defense training, techniques to disarm a "bad guy," and ethics training.

When Charlie traveled around to train police, he'd choose the biggest, baddest looking police officer to demonstrate how to subdue an assailant. He always told the officer, "Cross your arms when the pain gets too intense." Many of the police would laugh because Charlie was in his late fifties at the time. When Charlie had the policeman on the ground, though, they found new respect for him. After the self-defense training, he was also able to give ethics training and preach the gospel.

During our time of working with the police, we saw many officers receive Christ as their Savior. At the end of the

Several American churches supported our ministry in many ways, including supplying enough bibles so we could give one to every police officer at the end of the training.

session, Charlie gave each man or woman a Bible. After they received their Bible, the cadets and officers were free to go. I cannot tell you how many times they sat back down in groups and began to read the Word of God.

The ministry to the police was not without difficulties and trials, but we were very thankful for the opportunity that God had given to us. After four-and-a-half years, however, God closed those doors as quickly as He had opened them.

Chapter 10

Time to Build

Be assured and understand that the trial and proving of your faith bring out endurance and steadfastness and patience. But let endurance and steadfastness and patience have full play and do a thorough work, so that you may be people perfectly and fully developed with no defects, lacking in nothing.

James 1:3-4 (Amplified Bible)

When God closes one door it is often because He is ready to walk you through another. That was the case with us. Our ministry to the police was only one aspect of what God had called us to do.

One day our doorbell rang, and we opened the door to Ruth Montufar and her daughter, Karina. As we sat down in the living room, it didn't take us long to see that Karina was a little nervous and there was purpose in her visit beyond the small talk. Karina told us of her desire to start a school in Buena Vista, a very poor area of Chimaltenango, where her father had grown up. She asked if we would help make that a possibility.

This took us completely by surprise and we were not really sure what to say. As the conversation continued and she shared her heart and dreams, we realized that her vision was from the Lord. We had already planned to go to the States for two months, and we told her we would help her if she found a place for the school by the time we returned. Karina left our house happy and encouraged that day, but little did we know what our commitment meant for us.

We did not hear from Karina during the two months we were in the States. We actually didn't give the little school much thought until a couple of days after we returned to Guatemala. The phone rang early one morning, and Karina asked us to come and visit Pasitos de Amor (Little Steps of Love). We had no idea what to expect, but we were excited to go and see.

While we were in the States, Karina used all her savings to rent a classroom, make desks, and purchase teaching materials. She led us into the Pasitos de Amor classroom, and twenty five little four-year-olds and five-year-olds stared back at us. Most of the little ones were content with our entrance, but a few began to cry. They had never seen North Americans, especially North Americans as white as we are, and certainly not ones with braces and crutches.

After a little while, the tears dried. As we spent the morning with them, they became more comfortable with us, especially with Charlie. He has a way with children that makes them feel loved and secure, so it wasn't long until he had them laughing. We even received hugs and kisses as we told them goodbye.

On our way home, Charlie asked me what I thought Karina wanted us to do. I said that I didn't know, but I would ask her and find out. The next day I called her and got right to the point. I asked, "Karina, is this your school and you want us to help you, or is this our school and you want to work for us?" She replied, "This is your school, and I want to work for you!"

God had never given us even an inkling that we would one day help start a school. This took us completely by surprise. First, we reimbursed Karina, then, we began to make plans for the following school year. Our enrollment grew quickly, and after the first year, we outgrew that little room. We needed to move somewhere bigger, but where?

Pasitos de Amor, our first little school of twenty-five pre-kinder and kindergarten students, was housed in a one-room storefront. The kids were stuffed into that little room like sardines with Karina Montufar, their teacher and the school's founder.

It wasn't long until Karina's dad, Juan Miguel, had the answer to our dilemma. He owned property right behind our school. Several times, Juan Miguel tried to sell the property, which was his inheritance from his parents, but each time something got in the way of the transaction closing. At one point, Juan Miguel and a buyer were in the bank about to sign the papers when there was a problem with the buyer's financing.

The property lay dormant for several years, until the day came when God made it plain to Juan Miguel the reason why God kept closing the doors to the sale of his property. Once he understood, he contacted us and offered to donate his property if we wanted to build a school.

Gerizim Christian School, as it looks today. Our enrollment is 255 students for the 2013-14 school year, pre-kindergarten through ninth grade. The children are sponsored by individuals in the United States.

Charlie and I prayed about it and agreed that was exactly what God wanted us to do. Without a penny budgeted for building, we started the school project. To avoid overwhelming ourselves and those helping us, we built the school year by year, two classrooms at a time, adding a grade each year.

I remember being at the school during recess time in our second year. I was standing out on the playground watching the kids, when all of a sudden I realized the significance of something that God had spoken many years before. Remember the prophecy that was given to our son, Tommy and his wife, Holly: *I will have you building a place for Me, a place where I can send hurting, wounded and broken people, and you will be praying prayers of healing and deliverance over them, and you will be successful in all that you do?*

As I looked around at the fifty pre-kinder and kindergarten children, I realized that I was watching that prophecy come to pass. I knew that the hurting, wounded, broken people would be adults, but until that day, it had never occurred to me that they would be children as well. Once again, God had fulfilled his word at the *appointed time.*

When we added the third grade, we knew that we needed to change the name of the school from Pasitos de Amor (Little Steps of Love) to something a little more mature. It was pretty obvious by now that we were not going to just be teaching the little ones. The vision had grown to include junior high and high school.

Karina's mom, Ruth, was praying one day when God revealed the new name for the school by showing her *Deuteronomy 11:29*: When the Lord your God brings you into the land and helps you take possession of it, you must pronounce the blessing at Mount Gerizim.

Mount Gerizim, which means mountain of blessing, is where the Samaritans live in Israel. They have the smallest, most ancient, living ethnic community in the world. The Samaritans believe that when the Israelites first entered

Canaan more than 3,600 years ago, God told them to celebrate the event with a ceremony of blessings and cursings on Mount Gerizim. Moses ordered them to protect Mount Gerizim as a sacred mountain and worship there by making pilgrimages to it three times a year. Samaritans have kept these beliefs and traditions alive since that time.

When our school children walk through the gates of Gerizim Christian School, they enter an oasis—a place where they can set aside their hurts, worries and wounds for a time. Though many of our children are poor, many come from good homes where they are loved and cared for. We also have children who have been abandoned by one or both of their parents and raised by grandparents or other family members. Others have been sexually, physically, and mentally abused by fathers, grandfathers, brothers, and uncles.

For the first three years, Charlie was the school's director. This was a huge undertaking for him, since he was also supervising the construction of the facilities. You could see the effects of stress on him. If he could have just dealt with the children and not have had to also deal with getting the right staff in place, or the Ministry of Education, or the hundreds of other little details in operating a school, he would have been a happy camper, but it couldn't be that simple. There was much to do in getting the school established. Karina and her parents helped greatly by spending hours filling out legal documents and presenting them to the Ministry of Education.

Don't misunderstand– it wasn't all work and no play. Seeing the children's excitement in their new and different environment brought great joy to all of us involved. The days were filled with new and rewarding moments. Because they were so young and our ways as North Americans were so different, they had several learning curves.

One was how to use that white porcelain toilet. Karina walked into the restroom on the second day of school to check on one of her little pre-kinder students, and found him sitting on top of the commode tank with his little feet on the toilet seat. He had everything necessary aimed in the direction of the commode. She was a little shocked when she saw him, and so was he when she removed him from his perch and stood him in front of that white bowl with water in it. Thinking that he might not be the only one that needed some instruction, Karina altered her schedule a bit that day to include a lesson in toilet bowl use.

Trash was another cultural issue we had to address, because our students were used to throwing it on the ground. I am not sure how that custom got started, but it is deeply embedded in the Guatemalan culture. In our little oasis of Gerizim, that culture had to change. It took a while, but Charlie held firm to his no trash on the ground rule, and little by little they got the hang of it. One day a little boy ran up to Charlie yelling, "Mr. Charlie, I put my trash in my pocket." He was quite proud to pull all of the trash out of his pocket and show Mr. Charlie. After praising him for not throwing the trash on the ground, Charlie took him over to the trash can and explained again that this was where trash was to go, not in the pockets. More than once in those early days, mothers told us their kids came home with a pocket full of trash.

I will never forget the first time we loaded the children into our van and took them to the zoo. Most of those little guys had never ridden in a vehicle. When we arrived at the school the morning of our outing, we were shocked to find out that most of the moms had given their kids Dramamine to keep them from getting sick and throwing up. For the most part that worked, but not for all of them! We had not been on the road long when we heard someone yelling, "Stop!" We didn't make it in time and for the next ten minutes we cleaned vomit off a little girl and our van seat. Every few minutes we would hear, "Are we there yet?" The little ones had no concept of the distance from their little part of the world to Guatemala City. They had never made the trip before, even though it was only an hour away.

After three years, Ruth presented a solution for Charlie's stressful situation. She said, "I have the answer for you; let me be the director of the school!" Ruth had spent fourteen years as a home economics teacher at a private school, and she was ready to retire. Charlie's initial response was, "No." He explained to Ruth that if she were to become director, she would answer to him, and Charlie did not want to jeopardize our families' close friendship through any potential disagreements. After much discussion and Ruth's assurance that Charlie would have the final word if they disagreed on a matter, she took Charlie's place as director of Gerizim Christian School. She has remained so throughout these years, and our families are as close as ever.

Gerizim Christian School makes a huge difference in the lives of its students in Buena Vista, Chimaltenango, Guatemala. The children receive a quality education scholastically and spiritually. We are raising the next generation of believers in Christ, missionaries, responsible parents, and diligent workers who will enter a host of different vocational fields. We believe that eventually a president and his or her cabinet will come from our student body.

Chapter Eleven

The House On The Hill

Except the Lord builds the house, they labor in vain who build it.

Psalm 127:1 (Amplified Bible)

Remember when I shared Marsha Sanders' dream about our house on the hill? I want you to come with me now on another journey of faith. This journey will take you to the top of that hill in the mountains of Buena Vista, right above our school, Gerizim. Let's go; climb with me.

It was March, 2002. After two years as missionaries in Guatemala, we went back to the States to see family and visit friends and churches that were partnering with us. We visited Christian Faith Center Church in San Angelo during a prophetic conference. Denise Martinson, someone we didn't know very well, was seated behind us.

She only knew our children, and that we were missionaries in Guatemala.

During the ministry time Denise began to prophecy over Charlie. She said, *"Charlie, I see a "house on the hill" or a building. It is not real large, but very sturdy, nicely painted in good condition, blue gray front with wood trim. The front is off white or light. The road is steep but not rocky. Progress is slow but steady. The man on the road is carrying a large load of sorts. He does make it to the top, and there is great joy when he does. There are lush green fields on each side. The sun is very hot, yet pleasant, warming, challenging and comforting at the same time. It has something to do with Guatemala."*

The prophecy that God gave to Denise went hand and hand with the one about building a place for hurting, wounded, broken people, and also the one in the Marsha's dream about seeing our house on a hill.

The next night as we were about to sit down to dinner, Brenda Porter from Christian Faith Center Church rang the doorbell. Brenda had sat all the way across the building from us the night before and she knew nothing of the prophecy from Denise. Brenda was carrying a little tin house. She told us that she felt a little awkward, but that God had told her to bring us the little tin house. Brenda said that she had no idea why she was to bring it, but that she knew that God wanted us to have it.

The moment Brenda placed the little house in my hands, God reminded me of Marsha's dream in 1998 where she saw our *"house on the hill"* and the prophecy in 1999, *"I will have you building for me a place, a place where I can send hurting, wounded and broken people."*

The little tin house was designed and painted exactly as Denise had described the night before, blue-gray with wood trim and a thatched roof. But let me go on, because the story just keeps getting better.

Remember Randy Levens, the friend who told Charlie to go to the conference in Antigua and meet a man who would be very influential in our Guatemalan ministry? Well, a few months after we returned to Guatemala from the States, Randy sent an email: "God has given me the name for the "house on the hill." It is to be called *"Restoration Ministry Center."* That certainly sounded like God, since He had said in the prophecy in 1998 that He would make us *"restorers"* of people. So, from that point on, we began to call the house on the hill by its name, Restoration Ministry Center.

From time to time, people would ask us if we had bought the property for Restoration Ministry Center, or if we had a place picked out. Our answer to both of those questions was always no. There are a lot of hills in Guatemala, and every time I would pass one, I couldn't help but wonder if Restoration Ministry Center would sit there one day. We actually looked at several pieces of property, but they were either too costly or too far off the beaten path.

Because we were knee-deep in the construction of Gerizim School in 2005, and Charlie did not have time to travel around looking for property, Juan Miguel told Charlie that he would find someone else to do the looking. A few days later, Charlie, Juan Miguel and the finder of the property were climbing to the top of a hill with a beautiful view, covered in corn, and *lush green fields* on both sides. You could look down from the hill and see Gerizim School. Everything about the property was a perfect fit. We knew God had shown us the location for Restoration Ministry Center, and there was no need to look further. The land had been in the possession of one Guatemalan family for over fifty years. Not only was it the perfect hill, the price was perfect as well.

After years of believing in God's promise, the *appointed time* had *suddenly* come. Construction began within the month. It would take three years to build the Restoration Ministry Center. We were also still building Gerizim, which meant Charlie spent his days going back and forth from one construction site to the other, overseeing the work and purchasing the construction materials for both places. It was a huge undertaking for someone who had no prior experience in construction, let alone building it in a third world country where the ways are so different from what he knew. We were very thankful that we had waited on God's plan of putting our two ministries within ten minutes of each other.

The Restoration Ministry Retreat Center is often filled both with laughter and tears. There are tears because the ministry is to those who are hurting, but there's often laughter due to the joy of the Lord and the fun we have with our Guatemalan friends and our teams from the United States. Whether people are arriving or leaving, they always comment about the peace they feel on our mountain.

In September 2008, we walked through the doors of the newly constructed Restoration Ministry Center and into a ministry that God had foretold in 1998, many years before we would know about Guatemala and a house on the hill for hurting, wounded and broken people.

In the ensuing years at Restoration, we have seen God bless and minister to the hearts of His people, both Guatemalan and those from the States. It has truly been a place where people can come to find healing, whether it is emotional, spiritual, or physical. Throughout the years, people have come for a time of fasting and rest in the Lord, or for missionary, pastor and leadership conferences. Some have come just to sit on our back porch to visit over a cup of coffee and our famous banana bread, homemade by our precious Mennonite friends, Pat and Teresa Miller.

In our living room, we have seen people bow down with their faces to the ground as God poured out His Spirit upon them, confessing their sins, their wounds and their brokenness to the only One who can change them and make a difference in their lives. We have held them in our arms and prayed for them as they cried out to God. We have wiped their tears and shared their joys.

When people come to the House on the Hill, they often say, "It is so peaceful up here. God's presence is so strong." It truly is a place of restoration—a place where people can mend! Living in Guatemala and being a part of something that God has put together has been the most enjoyable thing that God has ever allowed Charlie and me to do. We have often asked ourselves, "Why us?" I am sure that has been the cry of anyone that has taken seriously the call of God upon his or her life. We know in our hearts that God could have chosen someone smarter and better equipped, but He didn't. He chose us. Not only do we have God to thank for believing in us, but also we have our sons, daughters, grandchildren, and a host of friends who have believed with us that *we would see the goodness of the Lord in the land of the living* (a reference to Psalm 27:13).

God continues to show us ways we can minister His love to the people in Guatemala. Every day our ministry provides clean drinking water and a nutritious breakfast drink to approximately one thousand students in five village schools. The government is supposed to supply these things, but the people who live in the villages are often forgotten. It has been a wonderful opportunity for us to share the love of Christ. We also conduct medical clinics in the villages and provide needed food for the elderly and widowed. There is no lack of ministry, if you have eyes to see and ears to hear.

Doors are still opening to us. God has recently fulfilled a long-held vision for Charlie to minister to the pastors in Cuba. I'm sure there will be other countries as well. We don't know where our entire destiny will take us, but we know that God will make it plain to us at *His appointed time.*

Chapter Twelve

Do You Want to Heal Me?

Bless the Lord, O my soul:
and all that is within me, bless His holy name.
Bless the Lord, O my soul,
and forget not all His benefits:
Who forgiveth all thine iniquities;
who healeth all thy diseases.
Psalm 103:1-3 (Authorized (King James) Version)

I want you to travel with me now to another *appointed time*. Remember the twenty-eight oak trees in our back yard in Cross Plains? I want to take you back to that time, January, 1985, to be exact. Charlie and I were able to attend the James Robison Bible Conference in Fort Worth that year. We were so excited to be there. There is just nothing like being under one roof worshiping with thousands of God's people. Some of our favorite speakers were there.

There is very little that I enjoy more than a good conference, but I was soon to find out that I wasn't there simply to enjoy the speakers, worship with other believers, and buy new books at the book table. God was going to do something this time that would catch me really off-guard. It may catch you a little off-guard too. This can be a good thing, because often we are a little too guarded when it comes to God.

The conference was different than the other James Robison conferences we had attended. We were introduced to a new speaker, John Wimber, about whom we knew nothing. John was there to help the Body of Christ minister healing to the sick. To be honest, we didn't really appreciate how he was going about it. People in wheelchairs and with braces, crutches and a host of other obvious physical problems were scattered around the room, but the only people being called out for prayer were those whose health problems could not be obviously seen. Now bear in mind, we had precious little knowledge of healing.

At the end of the second day, Charlie could not keep quiet any longer. When the session was over, he immediately began to tell me what he thought, pointing out that nobody seemed to notice all the people in wheel chairs, braces and crutches. He was not too happy about it, either.

I tried to get him to talk to one of the speakers, Dudley Hall, for whom we had a great deal of respect, as we did for James Robison. But like most husbands, he only wanted to complain to me.

I didn't know what to say other than remind him that we loved and respected these men, and they wouldn't have put someone on the program that they didn't hold in high esteem. At one point, I turned to Charlie and said, "If they call me up there, will you let me go?" He quickly replied, "I certainly will, because they won't call you up there unless they mean business." I thought my heart might beat out of my chest. I just knew they were going to call me up in front of all those people.

The conference ended without my being called up to the front. Though I was surprised, it was fine with me. It wasn't that I didn't believe in healing, I had just never considered it for myself. Interestingly enough, Charlie bought every book written by John Wimber at the book table before we headed home. That was the end of that, right? Wrong! We had only just begun.

We had been home from the conference for three days, and I was sitting at the kitchen table for my morning prayer time. Before I knew it, I asked God a question that had never once occurred to me to ask Him during thirty-six years of wearing braces and crutches.

I asked, *"Do You want to heal me?"* He responded very quickly, *"Yes, I do!"*

With that one simple question, I knew it was a done deal. My first conscious thought after God said, "Yes, I do" was, "But I don't have any shoes!" That is how real it was to me. At that time, my shoes had to be mounted on a metal stirrup that screwed into the brace. I couldn't just slip on a pair of shoes. After I quit laughing, I realized that I could happily go to the shoe store barefooted, if need be.

I had very little Scriptural knowledge of healing at that time, but I knew from that moment on, it was mine! I had received it. I also had a strong sense that it was for a definite time, because it was not going to be just about me but about a ministry that would come with it.

A month later, I was watching the 700 Club on TV. Ben Kinchlow had a guest that God had healed from a crippling disease. I saw the pictures of the gentleman before and after his healing, and heard the story of how he cried out to God to have mercy on him, just like blind Bartimeaus had done. I began to cry out those same words. In just a few minutes, Ben began to have a Word of Knowledge from the Lord, *"There is someone out there with metal crutches with arm bands; God is getting in the middle of that."* I knew that there were probably thousands of viewers that day that had metal crutches with armbands, but I also knew that those words were for me!

I didn't talk to God much about my healing that first year simply because I knew it was coming; I had no doubts. By then we moved to Snyder. One night, as I had finished washing the dinner dishes and was about to step from the kitchen into our bedroom, it was as if I had just picked up the conversation with God from the year before, *"How are you going to do it?* He replied, *"In your sleep!"*

Now I have to tell you, I could not have been more delighted. If I could have picked the way myself, I couldn't have chosen a better way than in my sleep. I was doing cartwheels on the inside. Charlie didn't have a clue that anything had just happened, because I was just as calm as a cucumber on the outside. I laid down in bed, picked up a Christian magazine and began to flip through it. Towards the back of the magazine, a story caught my eye immediately. It was a healing story! As I came to the end of the story, I almost came out of my skin. The last words of the story were, "And He healed me in my sleep!" Just ten minutes before, God had told me that He was going to heal me in my sleep.

Charlie's cousin, Raymond Harrison, his wife Diane, and

their children came for a visit about two weeks later. I had only met Raymond and Diane once before. When they arrived, Diane told me that their nine-year-old son, Brad, asked her what had happened to me. She tried to explain to him that I had had polio when I was a little girl. He was quiet for a minute and then said, *"You know, mom, wouldn't it be neat if Pat just woke up one morning and she was well."* Out of the mouth of babes! God had told me how He was going to heal me, and within two weeks He twice sent confirmation to His word.

Before I asked God if He wanted to heal me, I had never received a word from Him through anyone about healing. Since that day, though, God has given words, dreams, scriptures and visions about my healing to a host of people. I could almost fill a book with the prophetic words I have received. Once you take possession of God's word, there is something about receiving it that opens up the floodgates and allows you to receive other things as well.

When I sat at my kitchen table that day, I didn't know what a long journey I faced. I am not fond of waiting. I don't think most people are. I like to learn about something and then see it happen pretty quickly. From the beginning, God made it pretty clear to me that my miracle was not to be instantaneous. My healing is not just about being able to walk with two good, healthy legs. My

My parents, Tommy and Celesta Free, before their divorce, with my baby brother Dan. I was about seven, and still used regular wooden crutches.

healing is also about a ministry of healing and all of those who will be touched by it.

Most parents don't tell their kids about special events too far in advance; waiting is endless for children and every five minutes they want to know, "Is it is time yet?" As I write this in 2013, it has been twenty-eight years since God first told me that He was going to heal me in

Charlie and I were in the States visiting Daman, Karri Anne and our granddaughters when this picture was taken in 2013.

this life. It has definitely been a journey, a journey into faith and learning to wait earnestly for the promise of God without growing weary and throwing it away. I remember asking God several years ago why He tells me things so many years in advance. In my spirit, I heard Him say, *"So you can enjoy the journey."* I have found myself doing exactly what small children do when they know something special is going to take place. I ask my Father, "Is it time yet?"

Chapter Thirteen

Is It Time Yet?

For the vision is yet for an appointed time and it hastens to the end [fulfillment]; It will not deceive or disappoint. Though it tarry, wait [earnestly] for it, because it will surely come; it will not be behindhand on its appointed day.

Habakkuk 2:3 (Amplified Bible)

God gave me this Scripture in 1994, and it became the fertile soil wherein my faith would grow. It was not only the Scripture for the special, end-time ministry and everything else that was yet to come such as the house on the hill, but it is also the verse that I cling to for my healing.

Terry Macalmon sings the song *"How Long,"* which really ministers to my heart. I can't tell you how many times I have asked God, *"How much longer will it be?"* In fact, I have had time to ask a lot of questions in twenty-eight years. I can't begin to tell you all I have learned about healing, but in a nutshell, I will tell you that according to God's Word, He wants us well.

We only have to look at what Jesus did when He walked the earth. Over and over in the New Testament, we read: And He healed them all, and He healed them all, and He healed them all! Matthew tells us that Jesus not only died for our sins, but He died for our healing as well. He didn't just die for one part of man. He died for the whole man. *"And thus He fulfilled what was spoken by the prophet Isaiah, He Himself took [in order to carry away] our weaknesses* and *infirmities and bore away our diseases." Matthew 8:17* (Amplified Bible)

God has taught me a lot of things during these twenty-eight years. He has shown me a few reasons why His children have such a hard time believing that it is God's will to heal them. The main reason is that they don't know how much He loves them. They don't realize that they are sons and daughters of the living God. They don't know who they are in Christ and, more importantly, who Christ Jesus is in them. Therefore, they don't know what belongs to them, or what rights they have in the relationship with their Father.

Years ago, Charlie and I were away from home for a few days when our teenage son Daman called us and said, "Dad, do you remember that shotgun you *used* to have?"

Charlie said, "What do you mean that shotgun I *used* to have?" "Well, I traded it for a rifle!" Charlie hung up the phone and told me what Daman had done. Daman believed that if his father had something, it was his as well.

Did Daman act presumptuously? He had a strong relationship with his dad and knew his likes and dislikes. He believed trading the shotgun for the rifle would meet with Charlie's approval. And it did!

This is exactly how God wants us to act with Him. If God has provided specific things for us, He wants us to know, as His children, we have a right to them. They are ours. We are sons! We have a wonderful inheritance in Him.

The Word of God is clear about many ways that God's will affects our lives. We know with certainty that we can ask boldly for those things He has specifically promised without being concerned about whether or not they are God's will. However, when there are times we are not sure of God's will, we should pray that His will be done and not ours. We need to have constant communication with Him. When things are not clear to us, we need to diligently seek His advice on that matter.

Often, I ask God for direction in prayer when I am not certain of His will in the matter because I do not have a specific Bible verse to back up my request. I tell the Lord, *"This is what I am asking you for. This seems good to me, but if I am wrong, please feel free to tell me no. I want your will, not mine."*

There is no question what the Father's will is when it comes to salvation, healing, and deliverance. The Scripture leaves no doubt as to God's will: *"Beloved, I pray that you may prosper in every way and [that your body] may keep well, even as [I know] your soul keeps well* and *prospers." III John 1:2* (Amplified Bible)

God's children often have a hard time believing it is His will to heal them because they have chosen instead to believe the traditions of men, *"So for the sake of your tradition [the rules handed down by your forefathers], you have set aside the Word of God [depriving it of force and authority and making it of no effect]."* Matthew 15:6 (Amplified Bible).

That is a strong word. I have often wondered how much we have forfeited because we took the word of a preacher, evangelist or teacher over what God had to say in the matter.

The traditions of men have caused a watered-down gospel that renders it powerless. This leads to weak Christians who do not know how to believe God for the impossible or how to stand against their enemy, Satan, who wants them destroyed in every area of their life.

A few years back, I was visiting with a young lady and we were talking about the gifts of the Holy Spirit. When it came to the gift of tongues, she said, "I could never do that. It would hurt my dad too much." Her dad had been a preacher, and even though he was deceased, she felt more loyalty to his belief that tongues were not for today than she did to studying God's Word for herself. I have often asked God, "Is this just my tradition or am I being faithful to you and your Word?"

Many times I have told people to go back and read the Bible as though it was the very first time, without the drawing on the influence of anyone other than the Holy Spirit. *"My people are destroyed for lack of knowledge." Hosea 4:6* (Amplified Bible). We need to continually ask God to give us knowledge so that the lack of the truth will not destroy us.

Impatience is another reason why some of God's children have such a hard time believing that it is His will to heal them. We don't want to wait on anything! If it takes longer than we think it should, we throw it away and assume that God didn't mean that promise to be ours in the first place. Hebrews 10:36 tells us that we have need of steadfast patience and endurance if we want to receive, carry away and enjoy to the full what is promised.

Throughout all my *appointed times,* God has taught me to earnestly and patiently wait. Everything that God has ever said, He has spoken years in advance. The first time I heard Him speak to me about being a missionary, I was thirteen years old. I didn't see that word fulfilled until forty years later. It took twenty-two years to realize the special, end-time ministry, and He and I have been planning my healing and what we will do when it is manifested for the last twenty-eight years. But I am in good company; Abraham and Sarah knew what it was to wait. From the time that God told them about Isaac, twenty-five years passed before they held him in their arms. They also knew what it was to become impatient, thus Ishmael was born to Abraham's concubine.

Have you ever thought about Jesus having to wait on God's timing? Give this some thought. He came to save the lost, heal the sick, drive out demons, raise the dead, and preach the good news of the Gospel. He came to do the will of His Father. He didn't even start to do these things until He was thirty years old. All we know about His first thirty years is that He worked in a carpenter shop with Joseph, His earthly father, and yet He was in the very center of God's timing. To us, it seems like years were wasted. He knew exactly why He was here. The timing of His Father's will was His only motivation. Just the other day, God pointed out a precious Scripture to me that answered yet another question:

As he passed along, He noticed a man blind from his birth.
His disciples asked Him, Rabbi, who sinned,
this man or his parents, that he should be born blind?
Jesus answered, It was not that this man or his parents sinned,
but he was born blind in order that the workings of God
should be manifested [displayed and illustrated] in him.

John 9:1-3 (Amplified Bible)

I don't waste my time by sitting around feeling sorry for myself. God has given me a wonderful life, and I have shown Him gratitude by enjoying it. Sometimes I've wondered why I had polio, but it does not mean I think God has treated me unfairly. I have never asked God, "Why did you do this to me?" because I do not believe God made me sick. The Word of God tells us that Satan is the one that comes to kill, steal and destroy, not God. If polio doesn't fit that description, I don't know what does. Don't blame God for the things in your life that have been killed, stolen and destroyed. We have an enemy that hates us with a passion, and he is constantly seeking ways to destroy us.

John 9:1-3 does not mean that God wants us to be sick. After Jesus told His disciples the man was born blind was so the workings of God might be manifested, He didn't leave the man blind—He healed him and then put him on display! You and I and millions more have read about him. I would say he has been displayed pretty well, wouldn't you?

After I read this Scripture, I started thinking about things that we display. I like to display pictures of my family. My walls are plastered with sons, daughters-in-love and grandchildren. Why do I do that? There are several reasons, but the key reason is this: I display them because I want people to see them. I am proud of them and I want to show them off! When I saw this Scripture, God pointed out to me that this was what He wanted to do with my life, put me on display, so He can show off His work! This is not because I am so special, but because His work in me is.

I don't even remember when I wasn't spiritually pregnant with something from God. Pregnancy is a wonderful thing. I remember how excited I was when I first found out I was pregnant with each of our sons. I could hardly wait to hold them in my arms. Not a day went by that I didn't think about them, talk to them, pray for them and plan for them. By the ninth month, I was almost beside myself with the excitement of their arrival. Everything was in place. All that was left was endless waiting. Do you know how long a week can be if you are nine months pregnant? It can seem like forever! Every day I wondered how much longer it would be. I was tired and uncomfortable, and *so* ready to deliver those boys. Even though I was past ready, I knew without a doubt they were coming. It never once entered my mind that they would not be born.

That is where I am with my healing. I am in the ninth month of this pregnancy! But even though I am uncomfortable, and tired of waiting, these are the things that I know:

I know it will come in my sleep.
I know it will bring with it a ministry of healing.
I know it will not deceive or disappoint.
I know it will tarry (it will take some time).
I know I am to wait earnestly for it (expectantly).
I know it will surely come!
I know it will not be behindhand (it won't be late).
I know it will come on His Appointed Day.

Sometimes God waits until we think it is "too late." Mary and Martha certainly have a story of Jesus waiting until they thought it was "too late." When their brother, Lazarus, was sick, they didn't understand why Jesus didn't come immediately and heal him when they called for Him. When He finally did arrive, their brother was dead and they thought it was all over. Little did they know that God had a better plan. Even though we don't always understand, God doesn't require us to wait without a purpose in mind.

I have read Bob Sorge's wonderful book, *The Fire of Delayed Answers*, several times over the years, and each time I've been inspired by his insight and knowledge. Bob tells us that waiting on God purifies us, and the longer we wait, the more we are humbled and purified. He believes that we need to be totally humbled before we are ready to receive God's blessings, or we'll end up taking credit for God's gifts. Bob believes that God looks for those who are truly able to wait. If you have not read Bob's book, do yourself a huge favor and read it as soon as possible.

I waited patiently for the Lord to help me,
and he turned to me and heard my cry.
He lifted me out of the pit of despair,
out of the mud and the mire.
He set my feet on solid ground
and steadied me as I walked along.
He has given me a new song to sing,
a hymn of praise to our God.
Many will see what he has done and be amazed.
They will put their trust in the Lord.

Psalm 40:1-3 (New Living Translation)

I don't know if you are pregnant with a promise or not. If you are, and if you feel like your pregnancy is way overdue, I've found some words of encouragement: *God's delays are not God's denials.* God was right on time with Isaac. He was right on time with Jesus, and with many others in the Bible where God required a wait in their lives, and I am convinced that He will be right on time with me. Real faith causes us to enter into God's rest. If that is the case, then waiting on him should not cause us to doubt Him or live in frustration. He wants us to enjoy our journey with Him. Oftentimes our journey requires us to wait.

I love the story of Joseph. When he was a young man, God gave him dreams about who he would become and what he would do in the future. Because his brothers were so jealous and angry with him, they sold Joseph into slavery in Egypt and told their father that a wild animal killed him. The brothers even brought back Joseph's blood-soaked coat of many colors as proof. In his early years in Egypt, Joseph spent more than two years in prison because of a false accusation from Potiphar's wife. But God had purpose in it all. Joseph became the second most powerful man in Egypt; only Pharaoh was more powerful. The psalmist said of Joseph's ordeal, *Until the time that God's word came to pass, the word of the Lord tested him. Psalm 105:19* (New American Standard Bible)

Why did Joseph need to be tested by two years in a prison? Because of the call on his life! God had to bring him to a place where he could be trusted with his destiny. Because Joseph had once been a prisoner himself, he was now able to judge righteously. Joseph carried a word from God, in the form of a dream, for a long time. As he waited for the manifestation of his dream, the Scripture says that the word of the Lord tested him.

Often I am asked how I know that I am praying God's will. I know because God's Word is His will. I look to see what the Word of God has to say about a certain matter. If I want to know God's will on healing, I just simply remind myself that *Jesus bore my sickness and carried my disease* (Matthew 8:17). I see in God's word that *Jesus healed all who came to him.* We have no record of Jesus turning away anyone who came to him for healing. Jesus also never made anyone sick in order to teach them a lesson. That is just another of those *"traditions of men."* It has actually become a cop-out for many to not stand in faith, believing.

Let me ask you: How are you going to have faith to ask for something that you don't know is God's will? We must believe the word of God over the traditions of men, if we are to have faith. Don't look for a man-made safety net. Take God at His word when He says, *"And the prayer of faith will save the sick," James 5:15a* (King James Version)

Jesus healed them all, whether their faith was great or small. His Word tells me what His will is. It is just that simple. The traditions of men are what have made knowing God's will hard. God is not trying to keep His will a secret from you and me. He wants us to be able to follow Him to the fullest.

Every time I come to Him and talk about what He has promised me, He listens. Do you have any idea what happens when God listens to you? You need to know, because it will forever change your faith level.

> *And this is the confidence which we have in Him: [we are sure] that if we ask anything [make any request] according to His will [in agreement with His own plan], He* ***listens*** *to and hears us. And if [since] we [positively] know that He listens to us in whatever we ask, we also know [with settled and absolute knowledge] that we have [granted us as our present possession] the request made of Him.*
>
> *I John 5:14-15* (Amplified Bible)

If you will absolutely surrender your will to His will, He will move heaven and earth so you know what His will truly is:

Roll your works upon the Lord [commit and trust them wholly to Him; He will cause your thoughts to become agreeable to His will, and] so shall your plans be established and succeed."

Proverbs 16:3 (Amplified Bible)

You see, God only answers His own prayer.

Well, there you have it! As the old saying goes, "That's my story, and I am sticking to it." When I wrote this book, my healing had not yet manifested. You might think that I should wait to tell you about my healing until it has actually happened. What if it doesn't happen? But I would say to you, "What if it does!"

And since we have the same spirit of faith as he who wrote, "I believed, and so I spoke," we too believe, and so we speak.

2 Corinthians 4:13 (Revised Standard Version)

When God first told me about my healing twenty-eight years ago, I have to admit that it was pretty much all about me, even though I knew it carried a ministry with it. What I wanted back then would fit on a short list, but after all of these years of waiting, my list has grown much longer—*I want more!* I don't want it just for me anymore. I have a list of friends and family that I have asked God to heal too. The ministry that I saw twenty-eight years ago was small compared to what I see today. Thanks to this wait, my vision has become much larger. It continues to grow with every passing year.

If you have grown weary somewhere along the way with your wait and have thrown away the promise the Lord gave you, I encourage you to go back to where you laid it down, pick it up again, and continue your journey, *because it carries with it a great and glorious reward.*

Just remember, in the wait He is right there, very close,

My cousin Creg's wife, Teresa, visited Guatemala in May, 2013. We were in the prayer garden and she suddenly said, "I think you should have the children in the school pray for your healing." The instant she said it, I knew it was true. During chapel a few months later, I felt that it was time. The students eagerly gathered around me and prayed. Even after the time of prayer was over, students kept coming to me, wanting to pray individually and speaking words of encouragement. They, too, are waiting with me for the *appointed time.*

and even though you cannot see Him, He will make Himself known at His *appointed time.*

By sharing my journey with you, I hope your journey is made somewhat clearer. I simply want God to take what He has used in my life to encourage you in yours. It is my prayer that as you read *At His Appointed Time,* you find *your* appointed times, too. My desire is that you draw closer to the Savior because you took this journey with me. If you continue to trust God, at the *appointed time* His promises to you will *suddenly* be manifested.

I remain confident of this: I will see the goodness of the Lord in the land of the living. Wait for the Lord; be strong and take heart and wait for the Lord.

Psalm 27:13-14 (New International Version)

P.S. If my healing takes place before this book is published, I will add a final chapter. If my healing comes afterward, look for the sequel, *Healed at His Appointed Time.*

Blessed is she who believed that there would be a fulfillment of the things that were spoken to her from the Lord.

Luke 1:45 (New International Version)

Chapter Fourteen

Salvation Is Yours for the Asking

Now get to your feet! For I have appeared to you to appoint you to serve as my servant and witness. You are to tell the world what you have seen and what I will show you in the future. And I will rescue you from both your own people and the Gentiles. Yes, I am sending you to the Gentiles to open their eyes, so they may turn from darkness to light and from the power of Satan to God. Then they will receive forgiveness for their sins and be given a place among God's people, who are set apart by faith in me.

*Acts 26:16, 18 (*New Living Translation)

Before you lay down this book, I want to give you the opportunity to receive Jesus as your Savior, if you haven't already. We will share a few scriptures to help you understand the decision you are about to make, and then we will pray together.

Long ago God spoke many times and in many ways to our ancestors through the prophets. And now in these final days, He has spoken to us through His Son. God promised everything to the Son as an inheritance, and through the Son he created the universe.

Hebrews 1:1-2 (New Living Translation)

For everyone has sinned; we all fall short of God's glorious standard.

Romans 3:23 (New Living Translation)

Jesus replied, "I tell you the truth, unless you are born again, you cannot see the Kingdom of God."

John 3:3 (New Living Translation)

For God so loved the world that He gave His one and only Son, that whoever believes in Him shall not perish but have eternal life. For God did not send His Son into the world to condemn the world, but to save the world through Him. Whoever believes in Him is not condemned, but whoever does not believe stands condemned already because they have not believed in the name of God's one and only Son.

John 3: 16-18 (New International Version)

For it is by free grace [God's unmerited favor] that you are saved [delivered from judgment and made partakers of Christ's salvation] through [your] faith. And this [salvation] is not of yourselves [of your own doing, it came not through your own striving], but it is the gift of God; Not because of works [not the fulfillment of the Law's demands], lest any man should boast. [It is not the result of what anyone can possibly do, so no one can pride himself in it or take glory to himself.]

Ephesians 2:8-9 (Amplified Bible)

But everyone who calls upon the name of the Lord Jesus shall be saved.

Acts 2:21 (New Living Translation)

Jesus said, "Don't let your hearts be troubled. Trust in God, and trust also in me. There is more than enough room in my Father's home. If this were not so, would I have told you that I am going to prepare a place for you? When everything is ready, I will come and get you, so that you will always be with me where I am. And you know the way to where I am going." "No we don't, Lord," Thomas said. "We have no idea where you are going, so how can we know the way?" Jesus told him, "I am the way, the truth and the life. No one comes to the Father except through me."

John 14: 1-6 (New Living Translation)

There have been times when it has been hard to get my mind wrapped around how much love God has for me, when I can't quite grasp the full depth of His love. Then there are times when I can almost feel His breath on my face. I want to make sure you understand that your salvation is a free gift from God, and that gift has a name—JESUS. He tells us in His Word that He has prepared a place for us with Him one day. If you and I go there, it will not because we have been good and done good things in our earthly life.

Heaven is not for the good and Hell is not for the bad. Heaven is for those who received the free gift—Jesus-———and Hell is for those who rejected the free gift. God said that it was not His will for any man to perish. God has done everything possible for us to be redeemed. Don't ever lose sight of the fact that he loves you and wants you with him, if you want to receive his offer.

The ball is in our court, not in His.

If you want to receive Jesus as God's free gift of salvation, then I invite you to open up your heart to God and pray the prayer below with your whole heart. He is waiting for you to come to Him. Many think they have to clean up their lives before they can come to God for salvation, but that is just not true. If that were the case, then Jesus died needlessly. It is the blood of the Lord Jesus that washes away our sins as we surrender our lives to Him. Let's pray:

Father God, I come today to receive the gift of Your Son, Jesus, as my Savior. I am sorry for the sin in my life. (You may want to take time to confess to God what those sins are. Yes, He already knows, but there is healing that comes to our lives as we expose those sins verbally to God.) ***I ask you to forgive me. Fill me with your Holy Spirit in order that I might live a life that would honor you. I pray this prayer knowing that you have heard me, and that you have answered me. Thank you for saving me, and changing my life eternally. I pray this in the name of Jesus.***

Therefore if any person is [ingrafted] in Christ [the Messiah] he is a new creation [a new creature altogether]; the old [previous moral and spiritual condition] has passed away. Behold, the fresh and new has come!

II Corinthians 5:17 (Amplified Bible)

And I am convinced and sure of this very thing, that He Who began a good work in you will continue until the day of Jesus Christ [right up to the time of His return], developing [that good work] and perfecting and bringing it to full completion in you.

Philippians 1:6 (Amplified Bible)

Now that you have received Christ Jesus as your Savior, there is going to be a desire in your heart to mature in Him. I encourage you if you are a man or boy to find a seasoned Christian man to disciple you, and if you are a woman or a girl, likewise, find a strong Christian woman to help you grow in your faith.

Open your Bible daily and read what God has to say. If you are new in Christ, I would suggest that you start reading Matthew in the New Testament. It is important for you to find a group of believers (a church) to meet with on a regular basis. Because every church is not alike, pray and ask God with whom you are to meet. God will show you a place that lifts Him up, one that takes a strong stand in His word, not in the traditions of men.

May you be blessed as you experience God's Appointed Times in your life!

The Weaver

My life is but a weaving between my Lord and me.
I cannot see the colors; He worketh steadily.
Oft times He weaves in sorrow, and I in selfish pride,
Forget He sees the upper and I the underside.
Not till the looms are silent and the shuttles cease to fly
Will God unroll the canvas and explain the reasons why.
The dark threads are as needed in the Weaver's skillful hand
As the threads of gold and silver in the pattern He has planned.

Author Unknown

Chapter Fifteen

Lessons Learned

- God's "*suddenly*" doesn't mean immediately, rather it means "*at the appointed time.*" You may have to wait years for His appointed time, but stay in faith. Once the appointed time finally arrives, it will take place quickly because His word never returns void.

- Be determined. God will honor that.

- God is always with you and wants the best for you–whether you can feel His presence or not.

- Things may happen that you don't understand. Sometimes it may seem they are taking you in the opposite direction from God's promise. But God is faithful. He will use all those experiences to fulfill His purposes.

- God wants *you,* not all the things you do for Him.

- You don't have to beg, plead, or cry for God's promise. You don't have to feel that you aren't good enough or worthy enough. You don't have to go out searching for His promise. All you have to do is to remind God of what He said, thank Him, and wait for the fulfillment.

- Wait earnestly and patiently for the promise of God without growing weary and throwing it away. God's *appointed time* is coming.

- Hold on to His promises so you can walk in the destiny that He has mapped out for your life.

But as for me, I will look to the Lord and confident in Him I will keep watch; I will wait with hope and expectancy for the God of my salvation; my God will hear me.

Micah 7:7 (Amplified Bible)

The Author can be contacted at:

patricia@hisappointedtime.com

www.hisappointedtime.com

www.facebook.com/pat.reynolds.3363

Made in the USA
San Bernardino, CA
06 February 2014